SpringerBriefs in Architectural Design and Technology

Series Editor

Thomas Schröpfer, Architecture and Sustainable Design, Singapore University of Technology and Design, Singapore, Singapore

Indexed by SCOPUS

Understanding the complex relationship between design and technology is increasingly critical to the field of Architecture. The *Springer Briefs in Architectural Design and Technology* series provides accessible and comprehensive guides for all aspects of current architectural design relating to advances in technology including material science, material technology, structure and form, environmental strategies, building performance and energy, computer simulation and modeling, digital fabrication, and advanced building processes. The series features leading international experts from academia and practice who provide in-depth knowledge on all aspects of integrating architectural design with technical and environmental building solutions towards the challenges of a better world. Provocative and inspirational, each volume in the Series aims to stimulate theoretical and creative advances and question the outcome of technical innovations as well as the far-reaching social, cultural, and environmental challenges that present themselves to architectural design today. Each brief asks why things are as they are, traces the latest trends and provides penetrating, insightful and in-depth views of current topics of architectural design. *Springer Briefs in Architectural Design and Technology* provides must-have, cutting-edge content that becomes an essential reference for academics, practitioners, and students of Architecture worldwide.

Margherita Lasorella • Elena Cantatore
Yolanda Hernández Navarro • Fabio Fatiguso

Architectural Heritage Management via Digital Code of Practice

Springer

Margherita Lasorella
DICATECh Department
Politecnico di Bari
Bari, Italy

Elena Cantatore
DICATECh Department
Politecnico di Bari
Bari, Italy

Yolanda Hernández Navarro
Dpto. de Composición Arquitectónica
Universitat Politècnica de València
Valencia, Spain

Fabio Fatiguso
DICATECh Department
Politecnico di Bari
Bari, Italy

ISSN 2199-580X ISSN 2199-5818 (electronic)
SpringerBriefs in Architectural Design and Technology
ISBN 978-981-95-5105-7 ISBN 978-981-95-5106-4 (eBook)
https://doi.org/10.1007/978-981-95-5106-4

This Springer imprint is published by the registered company Springer Nature Singapore Pte Ltd.
The registered company address is: 152 Beach Road, #21-01/04 Gateway East, Singapore 189721, Singapore

If you insist and resist, you achieve and conquer.

Authors' Contribution

This book is written by Lasorella Margherita, Cantatore Elena, Hernández Navarro Yolanda, and Fatiguso Fabio. Lasorella Margherita (corresponding Author) and Cantatore Elena contributed to the conceptualisation, writing (original draft preparation), data curation, formal analysis, investigation and visualisation. Hernández Navarro Yolanda and Fatiguso Fabio contributed to the review, editing, and supervision. In particular, the contribution of each author is reported for every chapter of the book in the following.

Chapter 1: Towards an Integrated Digital Methodology for the Preservation of Architectural Heritage—Lasorella Margherita, Cantatore Elena, Fatiguso Fabio.

Chapter 2: Knowledge-Based Management of Historic Built Environment through Digital Approaches—Lasorella Margherita and Fatiguso Fabio.

Chapter 3: Ontological Approaches in Systematising Technical Knowledge in the Preservation Process—Lasorella Margherita and Cantatore Elena.

Chapter 4: The Digital Code of Practice for Managing Historic District—Lasorella Margherita and Cantatore Elena.

Chapter 5: Application and Validation of 3hD-DigitalCode to Pilot Cases—Lasorella Margherita, Cantatore Elena, Hernández Navarro Yolanda.

Chapter 6: Final Perspectives on Integrated Digital Strategies for Heritage Conservation and Management—Lasorella Margherita, Cantatore Elena, Fatiguso Fabio.

About this Book

The book is structured in three fundamental parts, each of which focuses on specific aspects related to the structuring and management of technical knowledge of the historical architectural heritage for the identification of conservation strategies.

The first part defines the scope of the study and contextualises the relevance of conserving the existing built heritage at the district scale. Specifically, challenges and opportunities related to the understanding and management of cognitive information in a multi-scalar and multidisciplinary context are analysed. The existing needs and gaps in the field are identified in detail, paving the way for the following sections. The first part consists of three chapters that provide: (1) a comprehensive overview of the conservation process from a multidisciplinary perspective, addressing current challenges; (2) an examination of knowledge-based management of historic built environments through digital methodologies; and (3) an exploration of ontological approaches for the systematic organisation and integration of technical knowledge within the conservation process.

The first chapter presents a comprehensive overview of the conservation process, emphasising its multidisciplinary nature and the need for integrated approaches. It highlights how diverse fields—ranging from architecture and engineering to digital technologies and heritage studies—contribute to effective conservation strategies. Current challenges, including data integration, interoperability, and the management of complex historical contexts, are critically examined to outline future directions for research.

The second chapter examines current digitisation techniques for building-scale digital acquisition, utilising methods such as digital photogrammetry and Virtual Reality.

The third chapter addresses theoretical and methodological challenges related to the management of information concerning the classification of existing built heritage, focusing on the identification of established standards and ontologies for geometric and semantic representation. Consequently, it explores the conceptual framework of knowledge essential for the preservation of large-scale historic buildings.

The second part is presented as a single chapter that examines a specific methodological and operational approach for the digitisation of the cognitive and conservation processes of historic districts. In particular, this section details the tools and methods underpinning the Digital Code of Practice developed for managing Historic Districts, as well as the semi-automatic derivation of intervention classes and priorities through a Decision Support System. This system was designed by structuring a logical-relational framework to qualify the built environment, utilising standardised digital models based on the CityGML standard and digital systems employing Virtual Reality techniques.

Furthermore, a modular structure has been developed to support a multidisciplinary information system. At its core are the geometric models of buildings, which are linked to thematic modules for in-depth analysis of specific knowledge domains. This semantic enrichment of digital models at the district scale enables the integration and storage of several information—including archival, documentary, historical, technical, and diagnostic data—thereby enhancing the geometric reconstruction of architectural artefacts and facilitating comprehensive technical knowledge.

The third part reports the application and validation of the digital code of practice elaborated for the management of the existing architectural heritage through VR-based expeditious approaches, as well as through the use of a multiscale and multidisciplinary digital information system for the analysis, modelling, and cataloguing of the chosen survey areas. In detail, the digital code of practice has been validated on two emblematic pilot cases with respect to the intrinsic criticalities related to the physical and regulatory obsolescence of buildings (number and size of rooms, lack of services and urbanisation systems, lack of maintenance activities, and/or rehabilitation interventions). However, the following pilot case studies were identified: the historic centre of Carovigno (Brindisi, Italy) and El Cabanyal neighbourhood (Valencia, Spain).

The outcome of the experimentation is presented in detail, demonstrating how knowledge can be effectively disseminated throughout all phases of the conservation process among the various stakeholders involved. Moreover, it establishes a critical link between institutional-scientific entities and public authorities during the planning and design stages of interventions aimed at the recovery of historic centres and urban areas, addressing key challenges related to physical deterioration and functional obsolescence.

Contents

About the Authors

Margherita Lasorella is Research fellow at the Politecnico di Bari (Italy). She has specific experience in the field of Virtual Reality techniques for the recovery and use of the built heritage, with particular reference to innovative range-based and image-based technologies applied to survey. During her PhD period, she enhanced her expertise in the field of multiscale digital information systems, focusing on the analysis, qualification, and management of architectural heritage.

Elena Cantatore is Professor Assistant in Architectural Engineering at the Politecnico di Bari (Italy). Her scientific work deals with the recovery and maintenance strategies of cultural heritage and historic built environment, focusing on the effects generated by natural processes and climate change. She has reached specific research goals in the use of VR-based and parametric CityGML-based models for the recovery and management of architectural Cultural Heritage. Furthermore, other scientific activities relate to the normative and scientific analysis of the terrorist phenomenon in Europe in order to set up, calibrate, and test algorithms for the assessment of the associated risk and the potential mitigation of strategies in real case studies.

Yolanda Hernández Navarro is Assistant Professor at the Polytechnic University of Valencia (Spain) with over 15 years of experience in the field of Cultural Heritage conservation and restoration, specialising in sustainable, accessible, and inclusive development. Her work spans three key areas: research, teaching, and public engagement, focusing on the conservation of both tangible and intangible Cultural Heritage.

Fabio Fatiguso is Full Professor in Architectural Engineering and Building refurbishment and requalification at the Politecnico di Bari (Italy). He is president of the national association of the Scientific Society of Architectural Engineering Ar.Tec. His research and scientific activity relate to building refurbishment and maintenance, with particular reference to material, technological and functional aspects, as well as to techniques and technologies for diagnostics and control. Other research lines are related to the development of immersive VR/AR environments and HBIM approaches for multi-level assessment and diagnosis of building characteristics and pathologies. Moreover, he is the supervisor of activities related to terrorism risk, coordinating the process of solutions inventory, the identification of criteria for compatible solutions in real-world contexts.

Chapter 1
Towards an Integrated Digital Methodology for the Preservation of Architectural Heritage

Abstract The conservation of existing architectural heritage requires a multi-level and multi-thematic approach for analysis and diagnosis, capable of systematically collecting and correlating architectural (buildings, churches) and urban elements (streets, open spaces), along with building components (walls, roofs) and service infrastructures (water, electrical networks). This process must comply with landscape regulations and support the prioritisation and coordination of intervention strategies. Traditional tools and procedures for developing recovery plans often reveal critical limitations in data interpretation, integration, and time efficiency. Conversely, recent advancements in IoT and digital technologies demonstrate that structured ontologies (e.g. CityGML, IFC) and information systems (e.g. geodatabases, relational databases) facilitate the organisation of technical knowledge and the definition of consistent relationships aligned with current regulatory frameworks. In this context, the proposed book aims to systematise existing technical information while addressing fragmented and inefficient procedures through parametric and virtual digital models. The book introduces a digital code of practice for the conservation and management of architectural heritage, utilising CityGML-based models integrated with a Technical Decision Support System (T-DSS) and streamlined VR-based tools. The approach begins with an analysis of methodological and technical principles for developing semantic information systems dedicated to the digital study, modelling, cataloguing, and management of built heritage.

Keywords Data integration · Heritage management · Digital conservation · Information modelling for heritage · Data-driven conservation

Within the field of conservation and management of architectural heritage, historic urban areas hold particular significance. As intricate components of Cultural Heritage, these areas embody overlapping layers of historical, cultural, and architectural value that require detailed analysis, in-depth understanding, and thoughtful valorisation. Their complexity arises from the integration of urban morphology,

M. Lasorella et al., *Architectural Heritage Management via Digital Code of Practice*, SpringerBriefs in Architectural Design and Technology,
https://doi.org/10.1007/978-981-95-5106-4_1

architectural typologies, and the intangible values embedded in the built environment, all of which contribute to their unique identity [1].

In this context, the architectural heritage represents a fundamental element of these historic environments. It constitutes a complex ensemble of historically layered architectural artefacts, characterised by distinctive construction elements. Over time, these structures have undergone significant transformations that have altered their original configurations, necessitating targeted interventions for recovery and restoration. These actions, driven by the need to adapt buildings to contemporary functions (such as integrating essential services and in compliance with safety standards), must be carefully balanced to safeguard their architectural authenticity and integrity [2]. Effective management of these environments is therefore crucial to ensuring the preservation and transmission of the historical, cultural, and architectural values that underpin community identity [3].

Recent natural disasters, along with anthropogenic events, have highlighted the inherent vulnerability and heightened exposure of the built heritage. These recurring threats increasingly call upon the scientific and technical communities to devise and implement comprehensive strategies for assessment, planning, and management [4–6]. The primary objective is to safeguard and preserve the built architectural heritage, acknowledging it not only as a valuable historical and cultural resource but also as a crucial element in community resilience in the face of environmental and anthropogenic challenges. Architectural heritage assets are especially vulnerable, owing to a variety of intrinsic factors linked to their nature and construction.

Several objective conditions contribute to the fragility of architectural artefacts: (1) the geographical context of the site in which the asset is located [7]; (2) the morpho-typological characteristics of the architectural structure [8]; (3) the degree of preservation or degradation [9]; (4) the intrinsic properties of the construction materials [10]; and (5) the historical layering of transformations and interventions that have modified the original construction system [11]. The complexity of these contexts is further compounded by the involvement of multiple disciplines and the coexistence of different temporal and spatial scales [12]. In such a scenario, the management of technical data and knowledge became a critical challenge, both in coordinating the various stakeholders engaged in the process and in addressing the distinct phases of preservation [13].

Consequently, the conservation and protection of historical heritage emerge as pressing issues, underscoring the need for protocols dedicated to the systematic analysis, organisation, and management of information. Such protocols are essential to support informed decision-making and enable the effective planning of mitigation and prevention strategies, thereby ensuring the long-term safeguarding of these irreplaceable cultural assets [14, 15].

Within the current regulatory framework, the absence of standardised preservation procedures is evident. This gap stems from the diversity of contexts and the fragmented nature of existing regulations [16, 17]. In this complex scenario, the conservation of architectural heritage stands out as one of the most challenging and inherently interdisciplinary tasks. Addressing it effectively requires an innovative approach that integrates technical expertise, methodological rigour, and advanced digital competencies. Reworking conservation processes thus becomes imperative, calling for collaborative efforts among experts from diverse fields, the development of flexible and adaptable methodologies, and the promotion of conceptual frameworks that are both regulation-compliant and sensitive to the complexity of historic districts. Furthermore, enhanced sharing and dissemination of technical knowledge are key to improving the overall management of architectural Cultural Heritage [18].

It is therefore crucial to establish a robust connection between the construction and conservation features, the morphological-typological characteristics of the existing built environment, and the diverse parameters defining its risk exposure [19]. Such a connection can only be achieved through appropriate methods of representation and systematisation capable of capturing both the tangible and intangible dimensions of heritage. To this end, the adoption of new codes of practice is indispensable, both in terms of the procedural and methodological frameworks and in the deployment and integration of advanced tools for acquiring and digitising the physical environment.

The conservation of architectural heritage requires a comprehensive, multi-level, and interdisciplinary approach to both analysis and diagnosis. This approach must enable the systematic collection, correlation, and management of architectural features (such as buildings and religious structures) and urban elements, including streets and open spaces. Moreover, it should encompass detailed information on the physical properties of building components (e.g. walls, roofs), as well as critical infrastructure services (e.g. water and electrical systems). Such an integrated framework must align with landscape conservation policies and comply with relevant regulatory standards, thus facilitating the effective prioritisation and coordination of preservation efforts [19].

Conventional tools and procedural protocols for recovery planning have demonstrated major shortcomings, particularly regarding data consistency, interpretability, and the extended time required for information processing. Against this backdrop, digital technologies have profoundly reshaped the traditional methodological framework for the study and conservation of architectural heritage, ushering it into a new digital era. Innovative approaches employing information models to analyse the existing built environment—capable of integrating and correlating diverse and heterogeneous datasets—have proven invaluable for the documentation, understanding, and managing architectural heritage [20].

Recent research and applications in the field of the Internet of Things (IoT) demonstrate that digital models based on structured ontologies (such as CityGML and IFC) and information systems (including geo-databases and relational databases) provide a more efficient framework for organising technical knowledge while ensuring coherence within regulatory requirements [21]. This comprehensive process necessitates the collaboration among various domain experts and the engagement of multiple technical and administrative stakeholders. Conservation planning integrates operational, conceptual, and instrumental tasks, addressing both intrinsic factors (morpho-typological characteristics, materials, construction techniques, architectural significance) and extrinsic variables (including urban transformations, social dynamics, cultural values, and economic implications) [22]. These aspects must be evaluated not only in terms of their performance and regulatory compliance, but also in terms of their contribution to shaping local identity.

Aligning the development of digital tools with the traditional phases of the conservation process reveals several critical challenges: (1) data heterogeneity, arising from the diverse formats of acquired datasets (.ply, .las, .collada, .ifc, .gml, .jpeg, .html, .pdf) [23]; (2) multidisciplinary information, reflecting the wide range of sources (documentary, historical, architectural, and diagnostic) each contributing different types of information [24]; (3) data interoperability, which is essential for enabling integrated and effective analyses across platforms and disciplines [25]; (4) data volume, requiring advanced computational management strategies [26].

Within this framework, this book arises from the need to systematise existing technical knowledge and to address operational gaps through an integrated digital approach. This approach complies with current standards and regulations while promoting the adoption of advanced methodologies for the conservation and management of architectural heritage. Specifically, it aims to systematise available knowledge while also defining methodological workflows to address fragmented practices through parametric and VR-based models. By analysing methodological and technical principles for semantic information systems, this book provides a robust theoretical foundation and practical applications for modelling, cataloguing, and managing architectural heritage in digital environments. It therefore serves as an essential guide for bridging traditional conservation practices with the opportunities of the digital age.

Accordingly, the objective of developing the digital code of practice is to establish a methodological-operational protocol that enhances the technical understanding of the existing architectural heritage. Specifically, the book proposes a digital code of practice for the conservation and management of existing architectural heritage through CityGML-based models implemented with a Technical Decision Support System (T-DSS), as well as through expeditious VR-based approaches. This process begins with the analysis of the methodological and technical principles for the development of semantic information systems for studying, modelling, cataloguing, and managing architectural heritage in a digital environment.

At the core of the methodological approach lies the systematic structuring of technical knowledge and the integration of rules within a digital model.

Specifically, architectural heritage is described through a set of defined parameters, translating its characteristics and related information into both qualitative and quantitative data. These data are subsequently used to construct logical and relational models that support analysis and informed decision-making. The digital code is designed as a dynamic digital environment, progressively enriched through the integration of additional relevant information frameworks. Its primary aim is to serve as a supportive tool for processes related to the rehabilitation of existing built heritage. While accessible to professionals across sectors, including conservation specialists, it is specifically structured to offer a methodological and operational approach tailored to public administrations, facilitating the identification of predictive strategies for the conservation of architectural heritage.

Through this framework, the book provides a comprehensive overview of both the semantic and geometric organisation underpinning the cognitive and conservation process, bridging theoretical and methodological foundations with practical applications in specific contexts.

References

1. Liang W, Ahmad Y, Mohidin HHB (2023) The development of the concept of architectural heritage conservation and its inspiration. Built Herit 7:21. https://doi.org/10.1186/s43238-023-00103-2
2. Wang Y, Jin C, Xu D et al (2024) Analysis of multi-dimensional layers in historic districts based on theory of the historic urban landscape: taking Shenyang Fangcheng as an example. Land 13:1736
3. Ornelas C, Sousa F, Guedes JM, Breda-Vázquez I (2023) Monitoring and assessment heritage tool: quantify and classify urban heritage buildings. Cities 137:104274. https://doi.org/10.1016/j.cities.2023.104274
4. Cacciotti R, Sardella A, Drdácký M, Bonazza A (2024) A methodology for vulnerability assessment of cultural heritage in extreme climate changes. Int J Disaster Risk Sci 15:404–420. https://doi.org/10.1007/s13753-024-00564-8
5. Blavier CLS, Huerto-Cardenas HE, Aste N et al (2023) Adaptive measures for preserving heritage buildings in the face of climate change: a review. Build Environ 245:110832
6. Briz E, Garmendia L, Marcos I, Gandini A (2024) Improving the resilience of historic areas coping with natural and climate change hazards: interventions based on multi-criteria methodology. Int J Archit Herit 18:1235–1262. https://doi.org/10.1080/15583058.2023.2218311
7. Lasorella M, de-Dato P, Cantatore E (2024) Web-based platform to collect, share and manage technical data of historical systemic architectures: the telegraphic towers along the Madrid-Valencia path. Virtual Archaeol Rev 15:1–18. https://doi.org/10.4995/var.2024.20341
8. Barrile V, Bernardo E, Bilotta G (2022) An experimental HBIM processing: innovative tool for 3D model reconstruction of Morpho-typological phases for the cultural heritage. Remote Sens 14:1288. https://doi.org/10.3390/rs14051288
9. Miran FD, Husein HA (2023) Introducing a conceptual model for assessing the present state of preservation in heritage buildings: utilizing building adaptation as an approach. Buildings 13:859. https://doi.org/10.3390/buildings13040859
10. Todisco P, Aufiero F, De Vito E, Nastri E (2025) Typological characterization and mechanical behavior analysis of historic masonry walls in the Campania region. In: Mazzolani FM, Landolfo R, Faggiano B (eds) BT—Protection of historical constructions. Springer Nature Switzerland, Cham, pp 436–443
11. Saisi A, Borlenghi P, Gentile C (2023) Between safety and conservation—procedure for the assessment of heritage buildings based on historic research. Buildings 13:2236. https://doi.org/10.3390/buildings13092236
12. Liu Y, Jin X, Dupre K (2022) Engaging stakeholders in contested urban heritage planning and management. Cities 122:103521. https://doi.org/10.1016/j.cities.2021.103521
13. Sugiyama G, Bourgeois I, Rodrigues H (2025) A holistic methodology for the assessment of heritage digital twin applied to Portuguese case studies. Digit Appl Archaeol Cult Herit 36:e00390
14. Hassan HM, Abdel Hafiez HE, Sallam MA et al (2025) Multidisciplinary approach of proactive preservation of the religions complex in old Cairo—part 2: structural challenges. Heritage 8:89
15. Hassan HM, Abdel Hafiez HE, Sallam MA et al (2025) Multidisciplinary approach of proactive preservation of the religions complex in old Cairo—part 1: geoscience aspects. Heritage 8:56

16. Wang Y, Jin C, Wang T, Xu D (2025) The interpretation of historical layer evolution laws in historic districts from the perspective of the historic urban landscape: a case study in Shenyang, China. Land 14:1029
17. Wardekker A, Wilk B, Brown V et al (2020) A diagnostic tool for supporting policymaking on urban resilience. Cities 101:102691. https://doi.org/10.1016/j.cities.2020.102691
18. Atzeni C, Colavitti AM, Cadoni S et al (2022) Cross-disciplinary approaches to the regeneration of minor historical centers: the case of Mogoro in Sardinia. Sustainability 14:14439
19. Gigliarelli E, Calcerano F, Cessari L (2017) Heritage Bim, numerical simulation and decision support systems: an integrated approach for historical buildings retrofit. Energy Procedia 133:135–144
20. Ascione F, Ceroni F, De Masi RF et al (2017) Historical buildings: multidisciplinary approach to structural/energy diagnosis and performance assessment. Appl Energy 185:1517–1528. https://doi.org/10.1016/j.apenergy.2015.11.089
21. Bertellini B, Gottardi C, Vernier P (2020) 3D survey techniques for the conservation and the enhancement of a venetian historical architecture. Appl Geomat 12:53–68
22. Zhou C, Dong X, Zou Y et al (2024) A historical building information modeling-based framework to improve collaboration and data security in architectural heritage restoration projects. Buildings 14:1431
23. Kong X, Hucks RG (2023) Preserving our heritage: a photogrammetry-based digital twin framework for monitoring deteriorations of historic structures. Autom Constr 152:104928
24. Delegou ET, Mourgi G, Tsilimantou E et al (2019) A multidisciplinary approach for historic buildings diagnosis: the case study of the Kaisariani monastery. Heritage 2:1211–1232
25. Martinelli L, Calvano M, Calcerano F, Gigliarelli E (2025) Visual programming language to support interoperability of geometric and data modelling in HBIM processes. SCIRES-IT-SCIentific Res Inf Technol 15:85–96
26. Mazzetto S (2024) Integrating emerging technologies with digital twins for heritage building conservation: an interdisciplinary approach with expert insights and bibliometric analysis. Heritage 7:6432–6479

Chapter 2
Knowledge-Based Management of Historic Built Environment Through Digital Approaches

Abstract The chapter presents an analysis of the existing digitisation techniques for data acquisition at the building scale, employing methods such as photogrammetry and Virtual Reality (VR) techniques. On the one hand, it explores the potentialities of image- and range-based digital models for assessing the state of preservation. More specifically, the discussion focuses on the main procedures currently available for the semi-automatic mapping of textured point clouds, textured polygonal meshes and orthoimages. On the other hand, the chapter pays particular attention to the use of VR-based digital models for the systematisation of technical knowledge. In this respect, it examines the role of virtual digital models in the conservation process, as well as their main characteristics as conceptually structured models for storing and relating technical knowledge.

Keywords Digitisation techniques · Range/Image-based modelling · Digital models · Virtual reality · Immersive technologies

2.1 From Scans to Conservation: The Digitisation Processes for Gathering Technical Knowledge of the Existing Architectural Heritage

This chapter analyses the principal approaches discussed in the literature for acquiring technical knowledge of historical building stock, both at the scale of individual buildings and entire urban districts. Within this framework, the rapid advancement of Information and Communication Technologies (ICT), together with the growing demand for intelligent systems designed to represent, analyse, assess, and enhance the existing heritage, has fostered the development of innovative methodologies for studying historical architectural assets. These approaches aim to support key processes such as conservation, valorisation, and management by enabling more effective data acquisition, integration, and interpretation [1]. In this context, the digitisation of architectural heritage plays a pivotal role, involving the coordinated

M. Lasorella et al., *Architectural Heritage Management via Digital Code of Practice*, SpringerBriefs in Architectural Design and Technology,
https://doi.org/10.1007/978-981-95-5106-4_2

use of advanced digital methodologies and tools to capture the physical environment to generate photorealistic three-dimensional models that accurately reproduce the spatial and material characteristics of built heritage [2]. The digitisation of architectural heritage complements and extends the traditional cognitive approach to heritage analysis. This process encompasses the key activities required for diagnosis and for defining potential intervention strategies. Specifically, it involves: (1) acquiring metric and colorimetric data through digital surveying techniques; (2) producing digital models, typically represented as textured point clouds; and (3) analysing the conservation status through the identification and mapping of principal degradation phenomena. Advances in digital technologies have fostered innovative methods for assessing and documenting the state of preservation of architectural heritage, thereby supporting more accurate and comprehensive conservation planning [3]. This has produced a significant transformation in the fields of diagnostics and assessment of historical and architectural heritage. Such progress has been enabled by the widespread adoption of advanced tools for environmental data acquisition, including laser scanning, digital photogrammetry, and panoramic imaging. At the core of this transformation lies the use of these tools, which allow the precise and efficient capture of the geometric and material characteristics of built heritage.

In this scenario, the main digital reality-based techniques used for processing three-dimensional models of historical artefacts are:

- Image-based approaches, commonly referred to in the literature as architectural photo modelling, rely on SfM (Structure from Motion) algorithms to generate three-dimensional representations of architectural artefacts from photographic images [4].
- Range-based techniques, which capture the real environment through terrestrial (TLS-Terrestrial Laser Scanning), mobile (MMS-Mobile Mapping System), and/or airborne (ALS-Airborne Laser Scanning) laser scanning, acquiring three-dimensional metric data (x, y, z) in the form of textured point clouds [5].

Three-dimensional image/range-based reconstructions often involve interactive procedures for architectural structures, where a limited number of reference points and geometric primitives are insufficient to describe the 3D geometry. Consequently, in the development of digital models of complex architectural aggregates and artefacts which are characterised by intrinsic (construction techniques, materials, architectural and morpho-typological features) and extrinsic factors (state of preservation, environmental and geographical conditions) that may influence the level of operability, integrated approaches combining the two technologies have been developed and tested to ensure greater accuracy and completeness.

This integration aims to overcome the limitations inherent in each methodology, allowing for the acquisition and digital reconstruction of the architectural artefact in its entirety [1].

On the other hand, automatic matching procedures embedded in digital techniques are increasingly applied to objects that require highly detailed models in the form of dense point clouds, capable of capturing all surface discontinuities and morphological features with high precision. Recent scientific studies have assessed the comparative performance of 3D reconstructions generated by these techniques, revealing a considerable degree of overlap between point clouds produced through different approaches. These findings have led researchers to prefer photogrammetric approaches, particularly for setting up virtual environments intended for the dissemination, cataloguing, and valorisation of Cultural Heritage.

The growing adoption of photogrammetry is also supported by several practical advantages, including the relatively low cost of equipment (e.g. digital cameras), the straightforwardness of data acquisition and processing from images or video, and the increasing reliability of the resulting outputs, enabled by advances in Structure from Motion (SfM) algorithms. These factors have made photogrammetry an accessible and effective method for a wide range of professionals, including archaeologists, heritage specialists, architects, engineers, and researchers. In many cases, photogrammetric outputs now complement or replace range-based models, offering a flexible and powerful solution for three-dimensional documentation and representation of cultural assets [6]. These technologies facilitate the acquisition of highly detailed information related to historical and architectural structures. In addition, the emergence of multidimensional digital environments has enabled the effective management and integration of various types of data, including metric, geometric, diagnostic, and archival information. The combination of advanced data acquisition tools with the capability to create comprehensive digital representations marks a significant advance in the fields of preservation, analysis, and documentation of Cultural Heritage. These approaches have empowered professionals to capture intricate details with remarkable accuracy and precision, thereby enhancing the understanding and conservation of valuable heritage assets [7].

Simultaneously, in the field of recovery and conservation of existing architectural heritage, three-dimensional photorealistic documentation has become an essential tool for several key purposes: (1) recording and understanding the current state of conservation of heritage assets; (2) supporting the planning of appropriate intervention strategies; and (3) developing digital recovery plans or projects that enable the documentation of the diachronic evolution of conservation and maintenance activities [8]. Nevertheless, digital methodologies provide the ability to acquire and manage data on historic buildings continuously throughout the entire conservation process, enhancing the effectiveness and precision of heritage management. All these abilities are presented in-depth by Mendoza et al. (2023) [9], which provides a systematic review of the literature on the main digital technologies for Cultural Heritage conservation.

Moreover, reality-based digital models are valuable tools for the analysis of technical knowledge, as the integration of accurate metric information with a high-quality photographic documentation makes it possible to obtain information regarding the state of conservation of surfaces. Indeed, thanks to the acquisition of radiometric/colourimetric characteristics, methodological approaches have been developed to support the technical understanding of historical assets and aggregates with the aid of textured three-dimensional models.

Three macro applications derive from this potential within the conservation process:

- Cognitive, aimed at enriching the information-semantic level through the linking of multidisciplinary information structured according to specific targets to the three-dimensional model [10].
- Diagnostic, encompassing manual (CAD/GIS-based) and semi-automatic point cloud segmentation and classification procedures used for the recognition and definition of degraded surfaces. In particular, the semi-automatic approach involves the application of Artificial Intelligence (AI) algorithms, more appropriately Machine and Deep Learning (ML/DL), which process input data to inform subsequent decisions for the semantic segmentation of the three-dimensional model. Specifically, segmentation consists of grouping points (x, y, z) having common parameters; subsequently, the sets of points are classified through the association of specific attributes [11, 12].
- Monitoring the deterioration of stone surfaces, at predetermined time intervals, using and comparing three-dimensional datasets [13].

2.2 Virtual Reality Techniques to Support Documenting and Interpreting Architectural Heritage

Alongside geometric digital models, Virtual Reality-based (VR-based) digital environments have been increasingly explored for the development of interactive applications (e.g. virtual tours and digital reconstructions) aimed at enhancing the accessibility and understanding of built heritage. These immersive systems have proven valuable not only for dissemination purposes but also for building structured databases to support the technical knowledge, conservation, and management of architectural heritage [14]. At the same time, recent advances in digital technologies have led to the development of tools and methodologies capable of capturing geometric information from artefacts of different scales with high levels of accuracy and resolution. These innovations also enable the virtual reconstruction of such artefacts within immersive digital environments, providing realistic and detailed representations that can be used for analysis, interpretation, and communication purposes [15].

The virtualisation of the built environment can be effectively framed through the Reality Virtuality Continuum proposed by Milgram and Kishino (1994), which conceptualises a spectrum ranging from fully real environments to entirely virtual ones. This taxonomy establishes a continuum that links Virtual Reality (VR) and Augmented Reality (AR), underlining the potential for hybrid solutions that integrate physical and digital elements in varying degrees, and offering a theoretical framework for interpreting immersive representations of architectural heritage.

Within this continuum, the Real Environment (RE) or Built Environment (BE) is located at one end, directly opposed to the Virtual Environment (VE) at the other. Augmented Reality (AR) lies closer to the real end, as it prioritises the user's presence in the physical world while overlaying virtual information. Between these two poles is Mixed Reality (MR), which encompasses both AR, near the real end, and Augmented Virtuality (AV), closer to the virtual end of the spectrum.

VR, or VE, allows users to immerse themselves in fully digitalised spaces that closely replicate real-world settings yet remain independent of physical or geographical constraints. These environments support high-resolution, three-dimensional visualisation of architectural contexts and artefacts, allowing real-time exploration and interaction. Through such immersive experiences, users can engage deeply with reconstructed environments, benefitting from a vivid, realistic simulation that enhances their perception and understanding of the virtual heritage context [16, 17].

Interaction between users and the VE is made possible through both conventional interfaces, such as monitors, keyboards, and mice, and more advanced systems, including head-mounted displays, visors, and motion sensors. These technologies, the outcome of continuous innovation, greatly enhance the way users perceive and interact with digital environments, shifting the experience from simple observation to full immersion.

The visual effectiveness of such digitalised environments is further amplified through the use of Virtual Models (VMs), which enable the creation of accurate and faithful digital replicas of real architectural structures. These models can be explored remotely and support various levels of immersion, ranging from semi-immersive to fully immersive experiences [18]. Thanks to these features, VR has become a multidisciplinary tool with applications across diverse fields. In medicine, it is used for surgical training and cognitive or motor rehabilitation [19, 20]. The manufacturing industry utilises VR for design prototyping, virtual testing, and operator training [21]. In education and psychology, it supports experiential learning methods and treatments for disorders [22]. Finally, in architecture and Cultural Heritage preservation, VR enables the reconstruction and interactive exploration of historical spaces [23–25]. In these domains, the application of VR technologies proves particularly effective in facilitating the creation of immersive environments that support the virtual reconstruction of historical settings, architectural structures, and archaeological sites. Beyond their representational capacity, VR tools also function as powerful tools for communicating both the tangible and intangible values embedded in cultural artefacts, thereby enhancing interpretation, understanding, and appreciation across diverse user groups [26].

In the field of preserving Cultural Heritage, Virtual Digital Models (VDMs) have been explored at both the macro level (encompassing the built environment) and the micro level (focusing on architectural artefacts), as well as for the management of historical architectural heritage through the creation of visual databases [27, 28].

At the urban scale, authors have experimented with digital systems leveraging Virtual Reality techniques on established web platforms (such as Google, Bing Maps, OpenStreetMap) for seismic vulnerability analyses of Historic Centres.

The exploration involved testing the capabilities and assessing potential challenges associated with the approach and tools employed during the rapid and remote phase of gathering and analysing building characteristics [29].

At the building scale, Digital and Virtual Models play a crucial role in enhancing diagnostic and recovery efforts for Cultural Heritage [30]. Specifically, certain authors have explored the application of VR techniques to study architectural assets with distinct cultural value. They advocate for the incorporation of VMs at a precise phase in the conservation process, positioned between the survey phase and the creation of the three-dimensional parametric model. Indeed, VR represents an advanced digital tool and a repository of multidisciplinary information. It enables interactive engagement with digitised architectural environments, allowing users to explore, analyse, and manage technical data related to built heritage in an intuitive and immersive manner [14, 31, 32]. Conversely, the use of VDMs, structured digital models specifically designed through VR technologies, demonstrates significant potential in facilitating and coordinating information exchange among the diverse stakeholders engaged in the recovery and management of Cultural Heritage.

In this context, the VDMs are regarded as a valuable tool for an efficient analysis of the architectural asset under study. Within this model, multidisciplinary information, organised both thematically and in terms of data type, is systematically catalogued and localised. This facilitates the subsequent development of digital information models and systems [33]. These models serve as shared digital environments, enhancing collaboration across disciplinary boundaries and supporting informed decision-making throughout the conservation process [34].

VDMs are increasingly integrated into the heritage preservation process to enable accurate assessment of the conservation state of Cultural Heritage assets. They support the representation, management, and sharing of information through immersive, digitally mediated environments, offering a "virtual" approach to documentation and decision-making [35]. In the study conducted by Lasorella et al. [36], VMs integrated with information systems structured according to specific rules were employed as a supportive tool for expert users in the decision-making process related to diagnosis and subsequent recovery or restoration interventions. The authors outlined a streamlined methodological approach designed for remote utilisation and the application of technical knowledge in dealing with artefacts that are inaccessible or have low accessibility. This approach leverages VR to create a Virtual Model(VM), representing the digitised environment through advanced VR techniques and incorporating various information levels. At the foundation of these information levels lies specialised technical knowledge derived from the cognitive analysis of the architectural asset. This includes elements such as historical analysis, graphic elaborations, and diagnostic reports. This knowledge is intricately localised within the VM and is further catalogued and correlated within a relational database. Particularly, when digital systems are configured and structured correctly according to specific logical relationships and/or with the sector ontologies, they can provide crucial support to experts in the field during the analysis and technical knowledge phase of the conservation process. By harnessing the potential offered by these technologies, it becomes possible to enhance the technical knowledge of Cultural Heritage, making it accessible to diverse user groups. Furthermore, leveraging these technologies allows for the initiation of a digitisation process for existing architectural heritage.

The additional capabilities of VDMs are highlighted by the establishment of a Historic Digital Twin [30]. This involves enhancing the model's interoperability by incorporating active sensors and integrating it with other web-based systems [37]. At their foundational structures, VDMs can be structured as digital databases where information is interconnected both within the databases and across visualised scenes. Moreover, VDMs can be integrated with various information systems, including hierarchical, network, relational, and object-oriented database systems, to enable the digital storage and efficient management of data [38]. Furthermore, VDMs can be linked to Decision Support Systems, facilitating the correlation of technical information, organised as parameters, through multi-criteria relations and Artificial Intelligence algorithms, such as ML [39]. A systematic literature review on the applications of such VMs is proposed in [40]. From this, it becomes clear how the evolving immersive digital environments contribute to various applications, improving our understanding of existing built heritage. They enable precise planning and design of future scenarios, effectively representing, communicating, and preserving concepts and knowledge. This is accomplished through the contextual interaction of multiple users within a unified digital system. One of the primary strengths of these models lies in their capability to represent, utilise, and manage the real environment and associated information through the development of innovative methodological approaches.

The main purposes of VDMs are: (1) faithfully reproducing the real environment through computer graphics simulations, thereby generating a sense of immersion and interaction for the user with the surrounding environment, and simplifying the methods of accessing and engaging with it; and (2) establishing real information systems for the existing built heritage, ensuring the visualisation, implementation, and management of data and information. In this context, virtual environments can therefore contain specialised data, useful to different and relevant sub-fields, such as diagnostics information for defining the state of conservation and decay of architectural Cultural Heritage after specific tests.

References

1. Bertellini B, Gottardi C, Vernier P (2020) 3D survey techniques for the conservation and the enhancement of a Venetian historical architecture. Appl Geomat 12:53–68
2. Remondino F, Rizzi A (2010) Reality-based 3D documentation of natural and cultural heritage sites—techniques, problems, and examples. Appl Geomat 2:85–100
3. Brozovsky J, Labonnote N, Vigren O (2024) Digital technologies in architecture, engineering, and construction. Autom Constr 158:105212
4. De Luca L (2011) La fotomodellazione architettonica. Rilievo, Model Rappresent di Edif a partire da Fotogr, pp 19–30
5. Bitelli G, Castellazzi G, D'Altri AM et al (2018) On the generation of numerical models from point clouds for the analysis of damaged cultural heritage. IOP Conf Ser Mater Sci Eng 364:012083
6. D'Auria S (2018) Fotomodellazione con immagini da smartphone per la diffusione della conoscenza dei Beni Culturali. GEOmedia 22

7. De Fino M, Ceppi C, Fatiguso F (2020) Virtual tours and informational models for improving territorial attractiveness and the smart management of architectural heritage: the 3d-imp-act project. Int Arch Photogramm Remote Sens Spat Inf Sci 44:473–480
8. Mateus L, Fernández J, Ferreira V et al (2019) Terrestrial laser scanning and digital photogrammetry for heritage conservation: case study of the historical walls of Lagos, Portugal. Int Arch Photogramm Remote Sens Spat Inf Sci 42:843–847
9. Mendoza MAD, De La Hoz FE, Gómez JEG (2023) Technologies for the Preservation of cultural heritage—a systematic review of the literature. Sustainability 15:1059
10. Bertacchi S, Al Jawarneh IM, Apollonio FI, et al (2018) SACHER project: a cloud platform and integrated services for cultural heritage and for restoration. In: Proceedings of the 4th EAI international conference on smart objects and technologies for social good, pp 283–288
11. Grilli E, Menna F, Remondino F (2017) A review of point clouds segmentation and classification algorithms. Int Arch Photogramm Remote Sens Spat Inf Sci 42:339–344
12. Galantucci RA, Musicco A, Verdoscia C, Fatiguso F (2025) Machine learning for the semi-automatic 3D decay segmentation and mapping of heritage assets. Int J Archit Herit 19:389–407
13. Galantucci RA, Fatiguso F (2019) Advanced damage detection techniques in historical buildings using digital photogrammetry and 3D surface anlysis. J Cult Herit 36:51–62
14. Di Giulio R, Boeri A, Longo D et al (2021) ICTs for accessing, understanding and safeguarding cultural heritage: the experience of INCEPTION and ROCK H2020 projects. Int J Archit Herit 15:825–843
15. Manferdini AM, Russo M (2015) From survey to high definition representations of a continuous architectonical space. The case study of the Pomposa Abbey complex. DISEGNARECON 8:1
16. De Paolis LT (2012) Applicazione interattiva di realtà aumentata per i beni culturali. SCIRES-IT-SCIentific Res Inf Technol 2:121–132
17. Milgram P, Kishino F (1994) A taxonomy of mixed reality visual displays. IEICE Trans Inf Syst 77:1321–1329
18. Cipresso P, Giglioli IAC, Raya MA, Riva G (2018) The past, present, and future of virtual and augmented reality research: a network and cluster analysis of the literature. Front Psychol 9:2086
19. Alvarado-Omenat JJ, Llamas-Ramos R, García-García D et al (2025) Effectiveness of virtual reality in cancer patients undergoing chemotherapy. Systematic review. Int J Cancer 156:1419–1428
20. Gautam A, Asutkar S, Nagpure D (2025) Virtual reality in surgical training: trends and prospects. Multidiscip Rev 8:2025136
21. Guo W, Liu Y, Li Y (2025) Precision mechanical manufacturing and product appearance VR design based on environmental thermal energy control. Therm Sci Eng Prog 57:103124
22. Oje AV, Hunsu NJ, Fiorella L (2025) A systematic review of evidence-based design and pedagogical principles in educational virtual reality environments. Educ Res Rev 47:100676
23. Tang H, Zhang C, Li Q (2025) Assessing creativity and user experience in immersive virtual reality with cultural heritage learning. Int J Human–Computer Interact 41:8136–8152
24. Srdanović P, Skala T, Maričević M (2025) InHeritage—A gamified Mobile application with AR and VR for cultural heritage preservation in the metaverse. Appl Sci 15:257
25. Sanfilippo F, Tataru M, Hua MT, et al (2025) Gamifying cultural immersion: virtual reality (VR) and mixed reality (MR) in city heritage. IEEE Trans Games
26. Abukarki HJ (2025) Beyond preservation: a survey of the role of virtual reality in experiencing and understanding historical architectural spaces. Buildings 15:1531
27. Ferrari F, Medici M (2017) The virtual experience for cultural heritage: methods and tools comparison for Geguti Palace in Kutaisi, Georgia. In: Multidisciplinary digital publishing institute proceedings, p 932
28. Harun NZ, Mahadzir SY (2021) 360 virtual tour of the traditional Malay house as an effort for cultural heritage preservation. In: IOP Conf Series Earth Environ Science, vol 764, p 012010

29. Columbro C, Eudave RR, Ferreira TM et al (2022) On the use of web mapping platforms to support the seismic vulnerability assessment of old urban areas. Remote Sens 14:1424
30. Sugiyama G, Bourgeois I, Rodrigues H (2025) A holistic methodology for the assessment of heritage digital twin applied to Portuguese case studies. Digit Appl Archaeol Cult Herit 36:e00390
31. Comes R, Neamțu C, Buna ZL et al (2020) Enhancing accessibility to cultural heritage through digital content and virtual reality: a case study of the Sarmizegetusa Regia UNESCO site. J Anc Hist Archaeol 7:124–139
32. Maiellaro N, Varasano A, Capotorto S (2018) Digital data, virtual tours, and 3D models integration using an open-source platform. In: International conference on VR technologies in cultural heritage. Springer, pp 148–164
33. Trizio I, Savini F, Giannangeli A et al (2019) Versatil tools: digital survey and virtual reality for documentation, analysis and fruition of cultural heritage in seismic areas. Int Arch Photogramm Remote Sens Spat Inf Sci 42:377–384
34. Banfi F (2020) HBIM, 3D drawing and virtual reality for archaeological sites and ancient ruins. Virtual Archaeol Rev 11:16–33
35. Cantatore E, Lasorella M, Fatiguso F (2020) Virtual reality to support technical knowledge in cultural heritage. The case study of cryptoporticus in the archaeological site of Egnatia (Italy). Int Arch Photogramm Remote Sens Spat Inf Sci 44:465–472
36. Lasorella M, Cantatore E, Fatiguso F (2021) Smart approaches to enhance technical knowledge of in/low-accessible heritage. SCIRES-IT-SCIentific Res Inf Technol 11:97–112
37. Trizio I, Savini F, Ruggieri A, Fabbrocino G (2021) Digital environment for remote visual inspection and condition assessment of architectural heritage. In: International workshop on civil structural health monitoring. Springer, pp 869–888
38. De Fino M, Bruno S, Fatiguso F (2022) Dissemination, assessment and management of historic buildings by thematic virtual tours and 3D models. Virtual Archaeol Rev 13:88–102
39. Lasorella M, Cantatore E, Fatiguso F (2025) Enhancing the recovery process for historic buildings through virtual environments based on panoramas integrated with informative system. In: Applications of immersive technology in architecture, engineering and construction. Routledge, pp 181–192
40. Wang J, Zakaria SA (2025) Design application and evolution of 3D visualization technology in architectural heritage conservation: a CiteSpace-based knowledge mapping and systematic review (2005–2024). Buildings 15:1854

Chapter 3
Ontological Approaches in Systematising Technical Knowledge in the Preservation Process

Abstract The chapter presents an analysis of existing methodological approaches aimed at investigating the management of information related to the classification of existing built heritage. The approaches are typically characterised by the use and the identification of existing standards and ontologies for geometric and semantic representation. Therefore, the conceptual basis of knowledge supporting the conservation of existing architectural heritage is examined. Particular attention is given to the qualification processes, with a focus on the parameterisation procedures for the built and urban environment. Moreover, this section provides an overview of the CityGML standard and its application in the context of architectural Cultural Heritage.

Keywords Built architectural heritage classification · Geometric and semantic representation, Parameterisation procedures · Digital heritage standards · CityGML

3.1 Semantic Structuring of Architectural Cultural Heritage Data

In recent years, increasing attention has been devoted to the role of structuring technical knowledge for the effective management of Cultural Heritage. This renewed interest particularly concerns the processes of identification, protection, and conservation of both movable and immovable heritage assets, encompassing historic buildings, archaeological sites, and cultural landscapes [1].

The knowledge and management of Architectural Cultural Heritage pose several challenges, primarily due to the complexity and diversity of the associated information. These challenges include:

1. The multidisciplinary nature of the data, which encompasses theoretical content embedded in both textual and graphic documentation.

M. Lasorella et al., *Architectural Heritage Management via Digital Code of Practice*, SpringerBriefs in Architectural Design and Technology,
https://doi.org/10.1007/978-981-95-5106-4_3

2. The heterogeneity of information formats and scales, ranging from written reports and photographs to drawings of varying structures.
3. The hierarchical organisation of information, which reflects varying levels of detail, from general overviews to highly specific descriptions.
4. The intricate granularity of data storage, particularly within existing digital and analogue archives, which is often hindered by the lack of a unified logical framework for structuring and managing such data [2].

Indeed, the analysis and management of built heritage face critical challenges arising from the integration of multidisciplinary, heterogeneous, yet complementary information. Addressing these complexities requires the adoption of formal and conceptual frameworks, such as ontologies. Ontologies play a crucial role across diverse scientific domains, including knowledge engineering, natural language processing, collaborative information systems, intelligent information integration, and knowledge management, as they provide structured models to facilitate consistent understanding and interoperability of complex data. Ontologies serve as fundamental tools for fostering a shared understanding of a particular domain, enabling effective communication among individuals as well as among distributed application systems with diverse characteristics. By providing a precise semantic representation of concepts and their interrelations within a specific field, ontologies play a pivotal role in structuring data and information. This semantic clarity not only facilitates information exchange and mutual comprehension among various stakeholders but also enhances interoperability between heterogeneous systems. As a result, ontologies support improved integration, retrieval, and management of information across complex and distributed environments.

Additionally, they facilitate more effective knowledge management across diverse domains [3]. Before examining the application of ontological structuring within the field of historical architectural heritage, it is essential to establish a clear understanding of the term *ontology* and its related conceptual foundations. This preliminary step is crucial for contextualising its role and potential within heritage documentation and management practices.

The term *ontology* has acquired multiple meanings depending on the context in which it is applied. Guarino et al. distinguish the use of the term *ontology* within two primary frames of reference: (1) philosophical, denoting a systematic relation of existence, and (2) computational, wherein what exists is what can be represented [4].

Starting from the axioms and meanings in [2, 4–6], an *ontology* can be defined as the formal specification of a shared and explicit conceptualisation. An explicit conceptualisation refers to an abstract model in which each object is represented through specific concepts, names, and explicit definitions. On the one hand, the name establishes the terminology associated with the object, while on the other, the definition provides the specification of the inherent meaning of the concept or relationship. Thus, the formally represented body of knowledge relies on a conceptualisation of objects, concepts, and entities that exist in a specific domain of interest, delineated by the relationships between them. Consequently, conceptualisation is embedded in the formal property of explicit specification through a defined language.

As a result, ontologies depict objects from diverse knowledge domains by means of:

1. Definitions, which identify the name of the specific entity and elucidate how the entities are interrelated.
2. Classes, which represent specific entities within the conceptual model (including objects and concepts).
3. Relations, which connect classes based on a defined structure (such as a network or taxonomy of classes and subclasses).
4. Attributes, which describe the characteristics of entities belonging to a specific class by defining their properties [6].

An *ontology* is a conceptual model that offers a structured and formally defined framework for representing a specific reality or domain. It functions as an abstract representation that organises knowledge through a semantic vocabulary composed of well-defined terms and concepts relevant to the domain in question. This vocabulary encodes the meaning of each concept and its interrelations, thereby enabling consistent interpretation and use. Ontologies can be expressed using various formal languages and notations; among these, graphical representations (such as diagrams illustrating classes, attributes, and relationships)—are commonly adopted to provide a clear visualisation of the conceptual structure and organisation embedded within the ontology. Depending on the type of language used, a continuum of ontology types has been outlined by Uschold and Gruninger [7], demonstrating the different approaches for structuring ontology models.

Within the domain of Cultural Heritage management, and as a response to its inherent complexities, a number of international standards have been developed to support the analysis, evaluation, and documentation of architectural assets. These standards are based on: (1) guidelines, which facilitate the comprehension of fundamental concepts organised into subcategories, fields, and relationships within the knowledge domain; and (2) vocabularies, which enable the development of standardised taxonomies and the structuring of technical knowledge.

The existing and most widely used standard for the representation and correlation of information in the field of knowledge of the built environment is the CIDOC-CRM ontology and its extensions. CIDOC-CRM (Conceptual Reference Model) is a unique conceptual reference model for Cultural Heritage. This conceptual reference model was developed by the International Committee for Documentation (CIDOC) of the International Council of Museums (ICOM) as a conceptual model and has become an ISO standard (ISO 21127:2006). The CIDOC-CRM is a formal ontology developed to support the exchange, integration, and harmonisation of information across heterogeneous sources within the Cultural Heritage domain. It provides a semantic framework capable of encompassing diverse documentation types, including museum collections, archaeological sites, architectural monuments, and archival records [8]. CIDOC-CRM is grounded in the principles of conceptual and semantic modelling, providing a standardised set of classes, properties, and relationships to represent key concepts and their interconnections within the Cultural Heritage domain. It enables the consistent and interoperable description of information related to objects, events, places, individuals, and other relevant entities. Specifically, the model is designed to support the cataloguing and documentation activities of institutions such as museums, archives, libraries, archaeological sites, and art collections, by organising information within a clearly defined semantic framework. The ontology is structured relationally, establishing links between physical objects (i.e. cultural assets), the events that have affected them over time, and the entities (such as individuals or organisations) that have interacted with them [9].

The structure of CIDOC-CRM is hierarchically organised, with classes linked through a network of properties and relationships. The model is intentionally designed to be extensible and adaptable, allowing institutions and communities to tailor it to their specific documentation and management needs. By standardising the representation of data, CIDOC-CRM fosters semantic interoperability across heterogeneous systems and institutions. In detail, the CIDOC-CRM conceptual model is composed of taxonomies structured around a standardised set of elements: (1) Classes, which define the core entities representing fundamental objects and concepts in the Cultural Heritage domain; (2) Properties, which establish semantic relationships between classes, enabling the model to describe how different entities are connected; and (3) Key concepts, which serve as the foundational constructs for modelling and interpreting heritage-related data.

CIDOC-CRM is designed to be extensible, allowing for the addition of specific classes, properties, and relationships to address domain-specific requirements or to facilitate integration with other standards and ontologies. Each CIDOC-CRM extension is specifically developed to tailor the foundational model to particular domains or sectors, thereby enabling a more accurate and context-sensitive description and management of data. These extensions enhance the specificity and adaptability of data modelling within their respective application areas.

Nonetheless, it is essential to ensure that the implementation of such extensions must remain consistent with the core structure of CIDOC-CRM. This consistency guarantees semantic coherence and supports interoperability among different systems and institutions involved in the exchange and integration of Cultural Heritage data.

In this context, it is essential to highlight one of the primary applications of the CIDOC-CRM ontology in the field of architectural heritage, specifically within the conservation process. This application was implemented in the MONDIS project, with the primary aim of creating an ontological framework for the automated analysis of the conservative state of built heritage, diagnosis, and potential interventions [10, 11].

The conceptual model was developed as the IT level of a mobile/desktop platform useful for the management of the knowledge required for the understanding and analysis of degradation phenomena affecting historic buildings. The MONDIS platform allows: (1) the acquisition and implementation of data in situ and/or on-desk, through the compilation of a report; (2) the modification of the implemented data and the integration of further information according to a controlled access system; (3) the validation of the technical knowledge collected in order to admit the data to the diagnosis section, as well as to the subsequent section of possible intervention strategies. Specifically, the input data are related according to the damage-centred conceptual model prepared on the basis of the Monument Damage Ontology [12].

The MONDIS ontological model uses existing taxonomies extracted from the scientific literature [11].

An additional ontological model, which takes into account the semantic structure of CIDOC-CRM, was developed in Acierno et al. [13]. This model was designed to represent Cultural Heritage throughout the entire conservation process. In particular, the model systematically integrates all phases of the conservation process through the use of parametric models based on the BIM approach, thereby promoting a coherent and coordinated management of technical and operational information.

In addition, another ontological model based on CIDOC-CRM is the CHEDO (Cultural Heritage Earthquake Damage Ontology) [14]. This model was developed to document earthquake-induced damage to historic buildings by integrating architectural, spatial, and environmental information. Thanks to this integration, CHEDO effectively supports the planning of post-earthquake restoration and reconstruction activities.

To address the above issue, glossaries, vocabularies, and classifications play a crucial role within the framework of heritage classification.

Specifically, the Getty Institute Vocabularies present a hierarchy of terms and definitions related to the heritage domain, with the goal of classifying works of art and architecture, names of artists or architects, and geographical categories.

One notable vocabulary within this framework is the Art and Architecture Thesaurus (AAT) [15].

The AAT is a structured vocabulary and thesaurus used for describing and indexing art and architecture-related information. It is a valuable resource for cataloguing and organising art and architectural materials in libraries, museums, archives, and other cultural institutions. In addition, AAT provides a standardised and controlled vocabulary for describing various aspects of art and architecture, including terms related to artists, art movements, architectural styles, materials, techniques, and more. It helps ensure consistent and accurate metadata and indexing for artworks, architectural structures, and other related artefacts. It is characterised by a semantic structure with a high level of granularity, such as to allow the definition of all the elements of a cultural asset. Finally, AAT is often used in conjunction with other standards and systems, such as the Getty Vocabulary Program's other vocabularies, to enhance the accessibility and retrieval of art and architectural information. The Getty Vocabulary Program is part of the J. Paul Getty Trust and provides several important controlled vocabularies for Cultural Heritage documentation.

3.2 Digital Standards for Representation of the Historic Built Environments: The CityGML Standard

The increasing challenges in addressing interoperability issues among existing urban and spatial databases, along with the need to integrate multidisciplinary data sources, have generated growing interest in the use of ontologies and standards for managing existing building assets. Ontologies provide a structured and standardised approach to knowledge representation, enabling a shared understanding of concepts and relationships within a specific domain. In the field of existing building asset management, they are essential for overcoming interoperability challenges and supporting the integration of diverse data sources. Recent efforts in managing technical knowledge related to Architectural Heritage have led to the systematic structuring of such knowledge, forming the basis for developing parametric digital models at multiple scales, from buildings to districts and urban areas. This section aligns with the scientific focus on shifting towards digital processes, methods, and models for community activities and services. Within this framework, models based on IFC, IndoorGML, INSPIRE, and CityGML standards are acknowledged as effective tools for representing and systematising information in architecture and urban planning.

Each of these technologies brings specific capabilities, at a building scale:

- IFC (Industry Foundation Classes) is a standard developed to facilitate interoperability in the construction sector, enabling the exchange and sharing of digital information among different users according to the BIM approach.
- IndoorGML (Indoor Geography Markup Language) is an open standard developed by the Open Geospatial Consortium (OGC) and is designed to ensure interoperability and data exchange between different software and systems. It provides a common framework for representing indoor spatial data and introducing the *cellular space* concept. It also allows the modelling of the geometry and semantics of indoor spaces, supporting interoperability and the exchange of indoor spatial data. In detail, it supports various applications such as indoor navigation, facility management, and emergency response planning.

Similarly, at urban scale:

- INSPIRE (Infrastructure for Spatial Information in the European Community) is an initiative aimed at creating a European spatial data infrastructure for the sharing of environmental and geographic information. It defines common standards and interoperability requirements for spatial data related to the environment. Promotes the sharing of geospatial data across European countries, supporting better decision-making in areas such as environmental management and policy development.
- CityGML is an OGC standard for the representation and exchange of 3D City Models. It allows for the representation of various aspects of urban environments, including buildings, terrain, vegetation, and transportation infrastructure,

in a standardised format. The CityGML standard facilitates the integration of 3D City Models into different applications such as urban planning, energy simulation, and disaster management.

These standards and ontologies contribute to a more comprehensive and standardised approach to managing spatial information in the context of architecture and urban planning. By incorporating these models into the ontology-driven approach, stakeholders in architecture and urban planning can enhance their ability to manage existing building assets effectively. The integration of ontologies and standardised models contributes to a more seamless and interoperable digital representation of architectural heritage, aligning with the broader digitalisation goals set by the scientific community.

Within this context, one of the key reference ontologies on the urban scale is the CityGML standard.

CityGML, an acronym for City Geography Markup Language, is an open standard designed for representing and exchanging 3D geospatial information related to cities and urban environments. Developed by the Open Geospatial Consortium (OGC), an international organisation dedicated to establishing standards for geospatial and location-based data, CityGML defines an XML-based data model and encoding for the representation of 3D city models [16].

The primary aim behind the development of the CityGML standard was to establish a shared definition and understanding of the essential elements, characteristics, and connections within a 3D City Model. Accordingly, the CityGML standard offers a structured and standardised approach for the storage and exchange of data related to urban objects, encompassing their geometry, semantics, and interrelationships.

In detail, the CityGML standard comprises two main components: a geometric-topological model and a semantic-thematic model [17]. The geometric-topological model concerns the spatial representation of objects, following the geometric classes defined by the ISO 19107 standard. Urban features are described as spatial aggregates, which can be combined into composite geometries and/or aggregated structures. For managing topology, CityGML employs the XML mechanism known as XLink, implemented through the Geography Markup Language (GML). Each geometric object is assigned a unique identifier, enabling it to be referenced within GML geometric properties. This approach facilitates the explicit representation of topological relationships between components of the urban model, while also preventing duplication of objects. Moreover, objects in CityGML can be represented with varying degrees of spatial dimensionality, depending on the type of element and the Level of Detail (LoD). The standard defines five Levels of Detail, ranging from LoD0 to LoD4, which reflect increasing accuracy and geometric complexity. This LoD framework supports multiscale modelling of urban features, allowing the same object to be represented at different levels of spatial abstraction, depending on the requirements of specific applications or visualisation contexts.

The second component of the CityGML model addresses the semantic-thematic aspect. This part of the model is structured using specific taxonomies and aggregation mechanisms, organised into a hierarchical system of classes. It incorporates semantic information to describe the functions and attributes associated with urban objects. These objects are modelled through a class hierarchy formally defined using UML notation. Within this framework, a CityGML model is semantically structured based on the following UML elements: (1) Element, representing the *Class*; (2) Attribute, which defines the properties associated with a *Class*; (3) Relationship, which establishes connections between two or more classes; and (4) Operation, is an executable process within the *Class*.

To each *Class* is associated a name, identifying the digitalised object (building, street, bridge), and its Stereotype which identifies the inherent scope of the class (*Type, FeatureType, Top Level Feature Type*). At the same time, a stereotype defines the extensibility mechanism that can be used to better identify the purpose of the model element to which it applies. They can be applied to the classes and relations of the conceptual model.

The hierarchy of types of *Class* can be identified in coherence with the type of *Relationship* that links classes:

- The relationship *Abstraction* links different classes having the same concept but describing it in multiple variations. The system of classes connected using *Abstraction* relation is the *AbstractClass*, and it contains the common properties of all the classes in the model (i.e. function, use).
- The *Inheritance/Generalisation* relationship links a *SubClass*, as a specialised class of the model to a *Superclass* which is a general one.
- The *Aggregation* relationship connects and associates two or more classes being a part of the aggregate class. The meaning of the relationship is *part of.*
- The *Composition* relation is a specialisation of the aggregation relationship, and it is useful for describing parts of a higher class. Here, the existence of the relationship is a function of the connected element. This relationship connects *ComponentClasses* to one *CompositeClass.*
- The relationship Association relates elements of different models.

Since its first release (v1.0), the CityGML standard has been structured into distinct functional modules, each focused on particular urban elements. These thematic modules have been progressively expanded in later versions of the standard (v2.0 and v3.0) [18, 19].

In general terms, the thematic structure comprises horizontal modules (*CityGML Core*, *Generics*, and *Appearance*) that are universally applied to all specific thematic modules. In addition, there are vertical modules serving as thematic extension modules within defined application-disciplinary domains constituting the urban environment. The main modules including *Appearance*, *Bridge*, *Building*, *CityFurniture*, *CityObjectGroup*, *Generics*, *LandUse*, *Relief*, *Transportation*, *Tunnel*, *Vegetation*, *WaterBody*, and *TexturedSurface*. The base class from which all thematic classes in CityGML are derived is the abstract class *CityObject*. As a result, all attributes and features of its subclasses—each pertaining to specific thematic domains and formally defined within the corresponding thematic modules—are hierarchically linked to the *CityObject* class.

Analysing version 2.0, the thematic structure comprises horizontal modules—such as *CityGML Core*, *Generics*, and *Appearance*—that are applicable to all specific thematic modules. Additionally, vertical modules act as thematic extensions within defined domain-specific applications that constitute the urban environment. The main modules include *Bridge*, *Building*, *CityFurniture*, *CityObjectGroup*, *LandUse*, *Relief*, *Transportation*, *Tunnel*, *Vegetation*, and *WaterBody*. All thematic classes in CityGML are derived from the abstract base class *CityObject*. As a result, the attributes and features of its subclasses—each corresponding to a specific thematic domain and formally defined within its respective module—are hierarchically linked to the *CityObject* class.

Furthermore, new modules—*Dynamizer*, *Versioning*, *PointCloud*, and *Construction*—were introduced. The *Construction* module, in particular, integrates the previously separate vertical modules—*Building*, *Bridge*, and *Tunnel*—all of which underwent thorough revision, along with the *Transportation* module.

The semantic-thematic structure supports multidisciplinary implementations of the CityGML standard through its extensibility. It enables the integration of custom attributes and elements into the standard schema for specific requirements related to particular domains or applications. The extension of the standard data model can be achieved in two ways. The first approach involves the use of the *GenericCityObject* and *_genericAttribute* classes, defined within the horizontal *Generics* module. This module allows an unlimited number of generic attributes to be assigned to each *CityObject* class, enabling the inclusion of additional properties specific to the urban model. Furthermore, each *CityObject* class can be linked to external resources via multiple *ExternalReference* elements, allowing associations with representations stored in other databases.

The second approach is the development of Application Domain Extensions (ADEs), which enable the introduction of new classes and properties into the CityGML schema. Unlike the Generics module-based method, this approach requires the creation of a dedicated XML schema file.

Both methods support the modelling and exchange of three-dimensional objects that do not fall within the predefined thematic classes or that require the integration of unstructured attributes not covered by the base schema [20].

Owing to the conceptual structure of the UML diagram (Fig. 3.1)—which underpins the extensibility of the CityGML standard—it is clear that the model is inherently well-suited for the development of Decision Support Systems.

Owing to its core features, the CityGML standard presents a valuable framework for the semantic modelling of built cultural heritage within urban contexts. Although it does not include specific modules dedicated to historic heritage by default, several studies have developed custom Application Domain Extensions (ADEs) to fill this gap. These extensions enable the integration of heritage-specific attributes such as historical stratifications, construction materials, functional changes over time, and conservation constraints.

The extensibility of CityGML ensures that such enhancements remain fully compliant with its specifications, thereby making the standard well-suited to represent the complex morphological and informative dimensions of historic buildings.

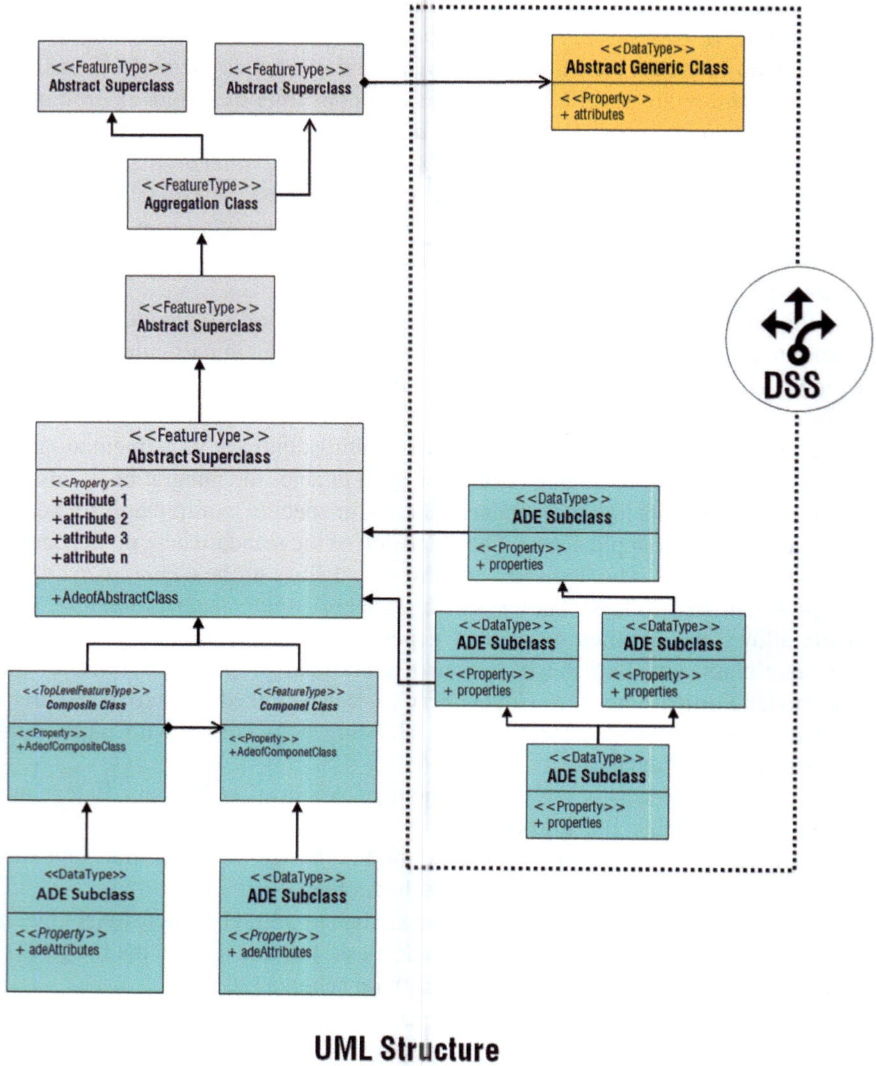

Fig. 3.1 A general example of hierarchical structures of *Class* types using the UML diagrams

These semantically enriched models provide important opportunities for documenting, analysing, and preserving architectural heritage, enabling applications at various scales—from individual buildings to larger architectural complexes—and across different usage types, including residential and special-purpose structures. Nonetheless, to adequately support conservation efforts, it is necessary to integrate structured ontological frameworks and decision-making processes that reflect traditional heritage management procedures.

In this scenario, the CityGML standard has been progressively adopted in the field of built heritage recovery and management, opening up new perspectives in cultural conservation and enhancement. Such developments are now shaping a rapidly evolving state of the art, in which CityGML emerges as a bridge between urban and architectural modelling and the digital management of existing built heritage.

Indeed, recent research studies have emphasised workflows and methodological strategies aimed at addressing and overcoming the main challenges involved in developing recovery plans for historic districts. These approaches are grounded in the use of systems and models defined by several key characteristics:

- Scalability, enabling the management of geometric data and information at multiple levels of detail, particularly supporting building-scale analysis within broader urban contexts.
- Multi-user access, allowing simultaneous engagement by diverse stakeholders, including citizens, public authorities, and technical professionals.
- Interoperability, ensuring compatibility of data from both technological and thematic-semantic standpoints.
- Structured semantic syntax, which combines geometric-topological and semantic-typological data within a hierarchical and relational organisation.
- Use of international standards, promoting open data sharing and facilitating cooperation across various platforms and institutions.

Building on the analysis of these concepts, Kokla et al. [21] developed a conceptual framework for representing architectural and urban elements within historic centres. Given the diversity of semantic and spatial dimensions involved, the authors highlight the need for a detailed ontological structure that can accurately describe historic architectural heritage from both semantic and geometric viewpoints.

This subject is further examined by Cecchini C [22], who proposes various approaches for creating a three-dimensional geographic digital archive of a historic district by integrating IFC and CityGML standards into a unified digital model. The parametric model, developed at multiple levels of detail, enables comprehensive utilisation and management of diverse information pertaining to individual buildings, while also facilitating effective control and oversight at the district level.

Based on these findings, Cecchini et al. (2020) [23] expanded the semantic representation of historic buildings by incorporating an energy-focused perspective. Specifically, they developed an Application Domain Extension (ADE) called ER_ADE (Energy Refurbishment ADE), which integrates two pre-existing ADEs—one dedicated to energy and the other to Cultural Heritage. This combined extension supports the monitoring and simulation of energy performance in historic buildings, aligned with the UNI EN 15603:2008 standard. The ER_ADE, linked to the Building thematic module of the CityGML standard, encompasses all aspects related to both the preservation of historic districts and their energy characteristics, facilitating classification in accordance with the Italian Energy Performance Certificate.

The authors in [24] enhanced the CityGML standard in terms of semantic and geometry to better organise and share historical data about lesser-known places. Their main aim is to protect the history of areas that are changing quickly.

Related to the interoperability aspect, more recent works about CityGML standard applied to historic districts focuses on the elaboration of methodological approaches based on the translation (IFC to CityGML, CityGML to IFC) of standards at different scales and/or on the integration of different ontological models (IndoorGML, CityJSON), also through the aid of the semantic web.

One of the first research works about the interoperability of BIM models and CityGML standards for historic districts is the work of [25]. Specifically, this work outlines an operational workflow for reproducing detailed historical buildings within a 3D city model by using data from image- and range-based acquisitions, with IFC serving as the primary standard compared to CityGML.

Subsequently, the experiences of [26–28] tested the highest degree of interoperability of the parametric model applying it for the maintenance of built Cultural Heritage.

Specifically, the authors examined and validated operational workflows, focusing on the processes of converting and/or creating a structured information system, identifying relevant features and their relationships within ontological structures towards the setup of a final CityGML-based model.

To this end, the authors in [27] developed an ontological structure that integrates CityGML- and IndoorGML-based models, enabling the creation and sharing of the resulting ontological model within a semantic web environment.

In detail, the IndoorGML standard was employed to establish connections between buildings and their surrounding urban context (streets, squares, open spaces), while the semantic web served as a tool for integrating the two standards. As a result, the authors developed a methodological approach aimed at creating a unified, standardised urban model.

Along these lines, the author in [26] implemented a similar multiscale data integration approach using CityGML standard encoding. The authors developed a semantic workflow based on CityJSON models to efficiently organise and manage the technical knowledge of the historic centre of Catania.

Moreover, the authors in [28] developed a workflow based on the CityGML JSON coding scheme, known as CityJSON, which enables automatic and dynamic updating of the semantic component to create diachronic urban models. A key feature of this coding scheme is the integration of temporal coding within the parametric model. Specifically, the authors introduced a structure called historical CityJSON, designed to build urban models that incorporate two-dimensional data—such as maps and historical cartography—along with attributes related to the historical and temporal dimensions of real-world assets.

Matrone et al. [29] developed a multiscale database (LOD 0 to LOD 4) for the management of historical heritage. The system integrates the IFC, INSPIRE, and CityGML standards within a web-based platform, enabling comprehensive access and organisation of heritage data across different levels of detail. In their study, Matrone et al. further advanced this approach by creating an integrated HBIM-GIS platform designed to support maintenance and conservation activities for historic built heritage in urban contexts, as part of the Main10ance project. The platform features an information database structured around a conceptual model that incorporates specific attributes related to the conservation status of historic buildings.

Similarly, Suwardhi et al. and Prieto et al. [30, 31] introduced a web-based platform accessible to both professionals and the public, designed to support recovery planning through collaborative and interoperable mechanisms. These platforms integrate building-specific data via the HBIM approach, starting from a CityGML-based urban model. Expanding upon previous approaches, the authors in [32] developed a top-down methodology for the semantic representation of historic centers, drawing upon established frameworks such as the CIDOC-CRM ontology, the CityGML standard, and the Getty AAT vocabularies. Their work highlights semantic enrichment by incorporating historical-identity values and regulatory data in accordance with ontological and semantic principles, thereby enhancing the conceptualisation of historic urban areas.

In Hidalgo-Sánchez et al. [33], a digital recovery plan for the historic centre of Seville was developed using a three-dimensional geographic information system capable of archiving data from analysis and technical assessments. This system was further enhanced by a semi-automatic procedure for the geometric modelling of architectural elements, systematically linked to qualified information within the geographic database.

The application of the CityGML standard to historic urban districts has also proven valuable for energy-resilient assessments [4, 20–22].

Several studies have proposed methodological frameworks aimed at qualifying historic districts and evaluating their energy performance, utilising urban parametric models structured to support interoperable, multiscale information systems that can inform policy decisions for sustainable urban development. In this context, Egusquiza et al. [34] and Prieto et al. [35] developed a web-based decision support system (DSS) integrated with CityGML to prioritise interventions at the block and building scale. Their system incorporates parameters such as primary use, number of façades, construction year, protection degree, energy performance, prior interventions, and physical condition to compute vulnerability maps using a classification based on combined value scales. These results formed the foundation for Egusquiza et al. (2020) [36], where the CityGML model was further enhanced with EFFESUS multi-criteria outcomes—based on an Analytic Hierarchy Process (AHP)—and aligned with ICOMOS guidelines on Heritage Impact Assessment. The method integrates energy savings, intervention costs, and cultural significance, and was validated through application to two case studies, demonstrating its potential as a comprehensive early-stage planning tool for selecting energy conservation measures in historic districts. Building upon these contributions, Cecchini et al. [23] introduced an approach that integrates parametric (IFC and CityGML) and energy models to generate a 3D representation and associated database for assessing the energy behaviour of individual buildings. Their system captures physical and performance parameters at the building scale and organises them within a web-based platform, providing a digital tool for managing historically regulated assets.

Egusquiza et al. [37] extended CityGML through energetic, Cultural Heritage, indicator, and dynamic domain classes as part of the EFFESUS methodology [38], enabling rapid assessment and selection of retrofit strategies in historic districts. Their approach focuses on typical building typologies and CityGML attribute hierarchies, combining geometric sub-component features (e.g. internal dimensions, facade orientation) with historical-semantic data (e.g. construction year, protection level) to evaluate energy performance in accordance with ISO 13790:2008.

Similarly, Cantatore et al. [39] proposed a CityGML-based methodology for the digital creation of energy-resilient plans, resulting in a 3D City Model accessible via the web for technical and administrative stakeholders. These studies underscore CityGML's effectiveness as a robust tool for the digital documentation, modelling, and preservation of built heritage. By offering a detailed and standardised 3D representation of historic urban environments, CityGML enhances the effectiveness of analysis, monitoring, and decision-making processes crucial to conservation strategies.

References

1. Bold J (2009) Guidance on inventory and documentation of the cultural heritage. Council of Europe
2. Khalil A, Stravoravdis S, Backes D (2021) Categorisation of building data in the digital documentation of heritage buildings. Appl Geomat 13:29–54
3. Fensel D (2001) Ontologies. Springer
4. Guarino N, Oberle D, Staab S (2009) What is an ontology? In: Handb Ontol, pp 1–17
5. Gruber TR (1993) A translation approach to portable ontology specifications. Knowl Acquis 5:199–220
6. Gruber TR (1995) Toward principles for the design of ontologies used for knowledge sharing? Int J Hum Comput Stud 43:907–928
7. Uschold M, Gruninger M (2004) Ontologies and semantics for seamless connectivity. ACM SIGMOD Rec 33:58–64
8. Doerr M (2003) The CIDOC conceptual reference module: an ontological approach to semantic interoperability of metadata. AI Mag 24:75
9. Oldman D, Labs CRM (2014) The CIDOC conceptual reference model (CIDOC-CRM): primer. CIDOC-CRM Off web site
10. Blaško M, Cacciotti R, Křemen P, Kouba Z (2012) Monument damage ontology. In: Euro-Mediterranean conference. Springer, pp 221–230
11. Cacciotti R, Valach J, Kuneš P et al (2013) Monument damage information system (MONDIS): an ontological approach to cultural heritage documentation. ISPRS Ann Photogramm Remote Sens Spat Inf Sci 5:W1
12. Cacciotti R (2015) Integrated knowledge-based tools for documenting and monitoring damages to built heritage. Int Arch Photogramm Remote Sens Spat Inf Sci 40:57–63
13. Acierno M, Cursi S, Simeone D, Fiorani D (2017) Architectural heritage knowledge modelling: an ontology-based framework for conservation process. J Cult Herit 24:124–133
14. Marín-Miranda MJ, Paleo UF, Redweik P, Gómez-Gutiérrez Á (2025) An ontology to describe the damage process to built cultural heritage triggered by earthquakes: the CHEDO model. J Cult Herit 71:114–126
15. Wielinga BJ, Schreiber AT, Wielemaker J, Sandberg JAC (2001) From thesaurus to ontology. In: Proceedings of the 1st international conference on knowledge capture, pp 194–201
16. Kolbe TH, Gröger G, Plümer L (2005) CityGML: interoperable access to 3D city models. In: Geo-information for disaster management. Springer, pp 883–899

17. Stadler A, Kolbe TH (2007) Spatio-semantic coherence in the integration of 3D city models. In: Proceedings of the 5th international ISPRS symposium on spatial data quality ISSDQ 2007 in Enschede, the Netherlands, 13–15 June 2007
18. Gröger G, Kolbe TH, Nagel C, & Häfele KH (2012) OGC city geography markup language (CityGML) encoding standard
19. Tatjana K, Kanishk C, Thomas HK (2020) CityGML 3.0: New Functions Open Up New Applications Abstract Zusammenfassung PFG – Journal of Photogrammetry Remote Sensing and Geoinformation Science 88(1):43–61. https://doi.org/10.1007/s41064-020-00095-z
20. Biljecki F, Kumar K, Nagel C (2018) CityGML application domain extension (ADE): overview of developments. Open Geospatial Data Softw Stand 3:1–17
21. Kokla M, Mostafavi MA, Noardo F, Spanò A (2019) Towards building a semantic formalization of (small) historical centres. In: ISPRS annals of the photogrammetry, remote sensing and spatial information sciences, pp 675–683
22. Cecchini C (2019) From data to 3D digital archive: a GIS-BIM spatial database for the historical centre of Pavia (Italy). J Inf Technol Constr 24:459–471
23. Cecchini C, Magrini A, Morandotti M (2020) The energy-oriented management of public historic buildings: an integrated approach and methodology applications. Sustainability 12:4576. https://doi.org/10.3390/su12114576
24. Ishar S, Zlatanova S, Yadav Y (2024) A data model for unrecognised historical Neighbourhood (case study: Telukbetung, Indonesia). Int Arch Photogramm Remote Sens Spat Inf Sci 48:247–254
25. Dore C, Murphy M (2012) Integration of historic building information modeling (HBIM) and 3D GIS for recording and managing cultural heritage sites. In: Guidi G, Addison AC (eds) Proceedings of the 2012 18th international conference on virtual systems and multimedia, VSMM 2012: virtual systems in the information society. IEEE, Milan, pp 369–376
26. La Russa FM (2023) A proposal for a parametric 3D city model semantic format. Nexus Netw J 25:481–489. https://doi.org/10.1007/s00004-023-00664-w
27. Malinverni ES, Naticchia B, Lerma Garcia JL et al (2022) A semantic graph database for the interoperability of 3D GIS data. Appl Geomat 14:53–66. https://doi.org/10.1007/s12518-020-00334-3
28. Vaienti B, Guhennec P, Di Lenardo I (2022) A data structure for scientific models of historical cities: extending the CityJSON format. In: Moncla L, Martins B, McDonough K (eds) Proceedings of the 6th ACM SIGSPATIAL international workshop on geospatial humanities, geohumanities 2022. Association for Computing Machinery, EPFL, Lausanne, pp 20–23
29. Matrone F, Colucci E, Iacono E, Ventura GM (2023) The HBIM-GIS Main10ance platform to enhance the maintenance and conservation of historical built heritage. Sensors 23:8112. https://doi.org/10.3390/s23198112
30. Suwardhi D, Trisyanti SW, Virtriana R et al (2022) Heritage smart city mapping, planning and land administration (Hestya). ISPRS Int J Geo-Inf 11:107
31. Prieto I, Izkara JL, Mediavilla A et al (2018) Collaborative platform based on standard services for the semi-automated generation of the 3d city model on the cloud. In: eWork and eBusiness in architecture, engineering and construction—proceedings of the 12th European conference on product and process modelling, ECPPM 2018, pp 169–175
32. Colucci E, Kokla M, Noardo F (2021) Ontology-based data mapping to support planning in historical urban centres. In: NP, CM, FL, et al (eds) International Archives of the Photogrammetry, Remote Sensing and Spatial Information Sciences—ISPRS Archives. International Society for Photogrammetry and Remote Sensing, Department of Environmental, Land and Infrastructure Engineering (DIATI)—Politecnico di Torino, C.so Duca degli Abruzzi 24, Torino, Italy, pp 39–45
33. Hidalgo-Sánchez FM, Mascort-Albea EJ, Kada M et al (2022) 3D GIS semi-automatized modelling procedure for the conservation of the PHiM: heritage municipal buildings of Seville (Spain). A new dimension for urban cultural data management. J Comput Cult Herit 15:1

34. Egusquiza A, Prieto I, Izkara JL (2016) Web-based tool for prioritization of areas for energy efficiency interventions in historic districts. In: REHABEND, pp 1755–1762
35. Prieto I, Izkara JL, Béjar R (2017) Web-based tool for the sustainable refurbishment in historic districts based on 3D city model. In: Lect Notes Geoinf Cartogr, pp 159–169. https://doi.org/10.1007/978-3-319-25691-7_9
36. Egusquiza A, Izkara JL, Prieto I (2020) 3d-gis models to support the co-creation of energy efficient strategies for historic urban environments. In: REHABEND, pp 409–418
37. Egusquiza A, Prieto I, Izkara JL, Béjar R (2018) Multi-scale urban data models for early-stage suitability assessment of energy conservation measures in historic urban areas. Energy Build 164:87–98
38. Egusquiza A, Brostrom T, Izkara JL (2022) Incremental decision making for historic urban areas' energy retrofitting: EFFESUS DSS. J Cult Herit 54:68–78. https://doi.org/10.1016/j.culher.2022.01.011
39. Cantatore E, Lasorella M, Fatiguso F (2021) Resilient improvement of historic districts via digital tools. The virtualization of energy retrofit actions using simplified CityGML-based plans

Chapter 4
The Digital Code of Practice for Managing Historic District

Abstract The chapter outlines the main steps and necessary tools within the methodological-operational approach for the digitisation of the cognitive and conservation process of historic districts. In particular, this chapter explicitly presents the tools and methods underlying the digital code of practice developed for the technical knowledge of the historical architectural built heritage, as well as for the semi-automatic derivation of intervention classes and priorities by a Technical Decision Support System (T-DSS). The code, called 3hD-DigitalCode, is developed through the structuring of a logical-relational scheme for the qualification of the built environment by digital models based on the CityGML standard, as well as digital systems exploiting Virtual Reality techniques. However, a modular structure has been conceived to support a multidisciplinary information system, maintaining the geometric models of the buildings as the central core, reflecting the correct dimension of the digitised architectural heritage (from building to district). In fact, all the thematic modules determined for the in-depth study of specific knowledge domains are related to the geometric core, thereby supporting a coherent structure of technical knowledge.

Keywords Digitisation · Built heritage conservation · Conceptual technical model
Multidisciplinary information system · Virtual reality · CityGML standard

4.1 Introduction

As presented in Chap. 1, the recovery process of historic districts is characterised by complexity, stemming from the need for comprehensive analysis and evaluation across various disciplines, scales and stakeholders. Such complexity arises from the intertwining of architectural, urban, cultural, and environmental factors, which must be simultaneously considered to ensure the preservation of cultural identity. Traditional conservation practices, although methodologically robust, often lack the standardised procedures and integrative tools needed to address the dynamic

M. Lasorella et al., *Architectural Heritage Management via Digital Code of Practice*, SpringerBriefs in Architectural Design and Technology,
https://doi.org/10.1007/978-981-95-5106-4_4

interactions inherent in historic urban environments. In this context, the chapter aims to define the digital code of practice as a strategic response to the complexities involved in the recovery of historic districts. By translating the well-established phases of conservation into a cohesive digital framework, this approach enhances both the precision and efficiency of decision-making processes. Furthermore, it promotes seamless interoperability among heterogeneous datasets and technological systems. Ultimately, the proposed framework supports the management and revitalisation of historic districts while respecting their cultural and architectural significance. For this purpose, the chapter provides a detailed and structured analysis that, on the one hand, systematises technical knowledge in accordance with conservation principles and sector regulations, and, on the other hand, outlines the phases and sub-phases of the methodological approach together with the necessary tools to support its implementation. This dual perspective ensures both the theoretical consistency and the practical applicability of the proposed framework, establishing a clear link between regulatory guidelines, conservation practices, and the digital tools required for effective intervention in historic districts.

4.2 The Structure of Technical Knowledge for Architectural Heritage in Historic District

The structuring of technical knowledge concerning to existing built heritage requires a systematic and multidimensional analysis of the tangible and intangible, regulatory and functional aspects that define its identity. This approach is essential to achieve both a comprehensive understanding and an effective management of architectural heritage. Within this framework, the present section illustrates the process of formalising technical knowledge and translating normative relationships into the Technical Decision Support System (T-DSS). The T-DSS serves as the conceptual foundation for defining the systems and models that constitute the digital code of practice, thereby ensuring the integration of regulatory requirements with conservation-oriented methodologies in a coherent and operational framework.

To this end, the analysis of existing built heritage can be systematically organised into four analytical categories:

C1. Environmental, Historical, and Cultural Values. This category involves the identification and classification of environmental, historical, and cultural values according to criteria established by preservation principles and regulations. It encompasses both tangible and intangible elements deserving of preservation, such as decorative friezes, traditional building techniques, historic building forms, and spatial configurations contributing to a sense of identity.

C2. Functional Obsolescence and Conservation Status. This category aims to identify and evaluate critical issues related to the structural, architectural, and hygienic aspects of buildings. This assessment includes: (1) categorising the technological and material characteristics of building components (masonry, fixtures, roofing, and systems); (2) analysing the geometric features of interior spaces (including the number of roofs, presence of openings, and room morphology); and (3) assessing the condition of non-structural elements (such as plaster and stone decay) as well as the functionality of building systems (including connections to networks and the efficiency of technological systems).

C3. Administrative and Regulatory Compliance. This dimension involves the collection and analysis of technical and regulatory data necessary to recognise the historical characteristics of buildings. Specifically, the primary administrative data include cadastral records, documented building modifications (such as changes of use, additions, demolitions, and superstructures), and the traceability of interventions over time.

C4. Recurring Building Types. The identification of recurring building typologies relies on the use of "building types" as representative models that describe and classify historic urban areas through consistent combinations of morphological, spatial, constructional, and material characteristics. This approach serves as an effective tool for the systemic interpretation of the built environment and for developing coherent strategies.

The conceptual model developed for this purpose is based on a hierarchical structure of synthetic parameters, derived from previous studies [1, 2] and subsequently refined to meet the methodological requirements of this book.

Building on this, the conceptual structuring of technical knowledge for historic districts requires three key elements: (1) identifying and categorising regulations, fundamental principles, and past experiences to extract geometric and semantic data, consistently defined using standardised terminology and requirements; (2) establishing the correct relationships and logical schemas among the identified data; and (3) organising the data into conceptual models structured according to the CityGML standard.

Specifically, the data within the conceptual model relate to four Informational Dimensions (InD), including: Preservation Principles (InD1), Sector Standards (InD2), a Glossary (InD3), and Ontologies proposed in the literature (InD4). These InDs are integrated and applied within the CityGML standard (InD5), which serves as a citywide reference framework.

According to InD1, ICOMOS (International Charters for Conservation and Restoration) provides criteria for the assessment of architectural heritage to support its conservation and management. The main tools developed by ICOMOS for understanding and assessing architectural heritage include guidelines and recommendations for conservation, restoration, and sustainable management, as well as International Charters [3, 4].

Regarding the process of analysis and evaluation of existing architectural building and urban heritage, which forms the relational framework of the T-DSS, it is aligned with the following standards and glossary, comprising:

InD2. UNI EN 16096:2012, for surveying the qualitative condition of buildings and urban elements (such as streets, squares, and open spaces).

InD2. UNI/CEN TS 17385:2019, for the quantitative assessment of the conservation status of architectural artefacts.

InD3. ICOMOS-ISCS Glossary [5], for the identification and classification of decay types.

As outlined in Chap. 3, ontologies play a fundamental role in knowledge management, serving as crucial tools for the semantic organisation and systematic processing of large volumes of information. The present research work considers three reference ontologies (InD4), selected for their relevance and complementary strengths in the semantic representation of Cultural Heritage.

CIDOC-CRM [6] was selected as a high-level ontology, widely recognised in the Cultural Heritage sector for its capability to model fundamental concepts related to the documentation, preservation, and history of cultural objects. Alongside it, CHADE (Cultural Heritage Application Domain Extension) was chosen as a sector-specific ontology, developed to extend the CityGML model by providing detailed descriptions of urban cultural heritage elements and enriching three-dimensional spatial models with semantic attributes [7]. To complete the framework, the conceptual model of SEH-SDB (Semantically Enriched Historical Spatial Database) was also included, facilitating the integration of historical, architectural, and cultural information within spatial databases [8].

The intrinsic ability of these sectoral ontologies to encode the semantics of data enables the automatic extraction, integration, and analysis of information, thereby optimising complex decision-making processes.

The conceptual-semantic model is structured hierarchically across three levels (Fig. 4.1):

1. Descriptors (D). These represent the raw data collected through surveys or archival research, primarily intended to document fundamental information such as construction period, building permits, intended use, and the maintenance condition of walls and roofs.
2. Primary Indicators (PI). These constitute the first level of derived data, enhancing the technical understanding of the descriptors by combining multiple derived indicators (nD).

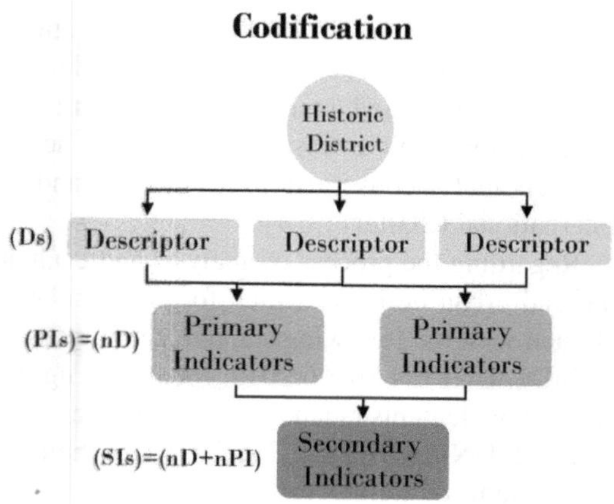

Fig. 4.1 Hierarchical structure of the conceptual-semantic model

3. Secondary Indicators (SI). Representing the highest level of derived data, these indicators are obtained through logical and/or mathematical processing applied either to the primary indicators (nPI) or to a combination of descriptors and primary indicators (nPI + nD).

In detail, the conceptual-semantic model organises the descriptors and indicators into seven analytical sections, grouped by thematic affinity and articulated across both urban and building scales, as follows:

- **S1. General Information (Section_Gen.Info)** collates all general data, including toponymic information (e.g. municipality, street name) and cadastral data (e.g. map sheet and parcel identifiers) (Table 4.1).
- **S2. Historical and Archival Data (Section_Historical_Archival_Data)** encompasses historical information (e.g. construction period, historical names of the property) as well as architectural data (e.g. construction type, building typology, number of floors, building height, function, and current use) (Table 4.2).
- **S3. Technical Knowledge Data (Section_Technical_Knowledge_Data)** provides information on the geometric, constructional, and material characteristics of each building element (e.g. walls and floors) within the architectural system (Table 4.3).
- **S4. Legislative References (Section_Ref.Legislation)** documents regulatory and administrative references associated with each architectural asset (Table 4.4).
- **S5. Architectural Elements (Section_Archit.Elem)** reports the main historical and architectural features of significant cultural and identity value (Table 4.5).
- **S6. Survey Status (Section_Cond.Survey)** describes the qualitative conservation level of buildings and urban elements, based on a visual assessment of their degradation state (Table 4.6).
- **S7. Conservation Status (Section_Qualification_Decay)** presents the results of a second, more detailed, quantitative analysis concerning the conservation condition of the buildings (Table 4.7).

Moreover, the relationships between Descriptors and Factors for each Primary and Secondary indicator are presented in Table 4.8.

From this perspective, the use of descriptors and derived indicators—categorised into Primary and Secondary—facilitates the identification of relationships between elementary data and higher-level information.

Table 4.1 System of data involved in Sect. 4.1—General Info. It classifies the data according to their Informative Dimension ("InD"), the "Level" used for structuring of conceptual-semantic model, and the corresponding CityGML "Class" (B Building, T Transportation, GA when the class is implemented with generic attribute) employed for modelling

Code	Name	Properties	InD	Level	Class
ID_B	Cadastral Data	Sheet, parcel, and subalterns	–	D	B/GA
ID_U	Urban Data	Sheet, parcel, and subalterns	–	D	B/GA
ID_T	Toponomastics	Avenue, Street, Square, etc.	5	D	B

Table 4.2 According to Table 4.4 in Sect. 4.2—Historical-archival data

Code	Name	Properties	InD	Level	Class
B_Cl	Building class	Building Type (castle, building, etc.)	5	D	B
B_Fct	Building function	Original use (residential, strategic, etc.)	5	D	B
B_Use	Building use	Current use (commercial, residential, etc.)	5	D	B
B_CP	Construction period	Construction period of building	5	D	B
B_DP	Demolition period	Demolition period of building	5	D	B
B_Ow	Building ownership	Public/private building	4	D	B/GA
B_St	Building state	Current condition (abandoned, partially used, etc.)	4	D	B/GA
B_PI	Presence of intervention carried out	Alteration of the original fabric	1	D	B/GA
B_TPI	Type of building intervention carried out	Building renovation, Static recovery, Raising, Conservative restoration, etc.	1	D	B/GA
U_Cl	Urban class	Classification of element (Street, square, etc.)	5	D	T
U_Fct	Urban function	Original use type of the urban element	5	D	T
U_Use	Urban use	Actual use type of the urban element	5	D	T
U_St	Urban state	Current surface decay of urban element	1	D	T/GA
U_PI	Previous interventions of urban element	Identification of transformations carried out	1	D	T/GA
U_TPI	Type of urban intervention carried out	Urban restructuring urban redevelopment	1	D	T/GA
U_PPI	Period/year of urban intervention carried out	Reference period relating to the execution of past urban interventions	1	D	T/GA

This structured approach allows for the translation of normative rules into formalised relationships, forming the logical foundation of a Technical Decision Support System (T-DSS).

A preliminary qualitative reconnaissance analysis is carried out at both urban and building scales, following the UNI EN 16096:2012 standard. Each urban and architectural entity is evaluated based on the properties associated with the B/U_CC descriptor, as detailed in Table 4.9.

Consequently, the type and priority of intervention on an urban scale are derived according to the conservation class of the urban element (Table 4.10) and the primary factor Urban Asset Type.

Specifically, for the building environment, according to Table 4.9, the classes of intervention (B_IC) is the ordinary maintenance, without priority, if:

$0 \leq [B\_CC] \leq 1$.

By contrast, a second level of in-depth quantitative analysis is required.

In this case, the state of preservation of the building is quantitatively assessed using the guidelines provided by the UNI/CEN TS 17385:2019 standard. This

Table 4.3 According to the Table 4.1, the system of data involved in Sect. 4.3—Technical knowledge data

Code	Name	Properties	InD	Level	Class
B_nFa	Storeys above ground	Total number of storeys above ground	5	D	B
B_nFb	Storeys below ground	Total number of storeys below ground	5	D	B
B_H	Measured building height	Maximum building height above the ground evaluated at the eaves	5	D	B
B_A	Floor area	Commercial area of the building	2	D	B/GA
B_WA	Wall area	Total extension of the wall	2	D	B/GA
B_Arf	Roof area	Total extension of the roof	2	D	B/GA
B_WiA	Window area	Total extension of window in each room	2	D	B/GA
B_Typ	Building type	Morpho-typology (palace, simplex, …)	1	D	B/GA
B_Str	Structural typology	Type of building structure (masonry, vaults, mixed building, etc.)	1	D	B/GA
B_WT	Wall type	Description of construction technique of wall and elements (e.g. compound wall with squared stone blocks)	1	D	B/GA
B_RT	Roof type	Description of construction technique for roof and elements + material of elements (e.g. vault in squared tuff blocks)	1	D	B
B_FiT	Type of building finishing layers	Description of materials for wall and roof finishing (e.g. mortar plaster walls; external bituminous finishing of roof)	1	D	B/GA
U_PT	Element type of urban paving	Surface finishing and material (e.g. paving in irregular cobblestones)	1	D	T/GA
U_PU	Primary urbanisation	Presence of any primary urbanisation	1	D	T/GA
U_TPU	Primary urbanisation type	Type of primary urbanisation (water, sewerage, electricity, gas, telephone, …)	1	D	T/GA

Table 4.4 According to the Table 4.1, the system of data involved in the Sect. 4.4—Legislative references

Code	Name	Description	InD	Level	Class
B_ChC	Cultural Heritage Constraints	Constraints defined by the Cultural Heritage and Landscape Code	1	D	B/GA

evaluation is conducted by correlating conservation data pertaining to individual building sub-components (such as masonry, floors, and windows) within the semantic-conceptual framework adopted for the definition of Primary Indicators (Sect. 4.7).

Table 4.5 According to the Table 4.1, the system of data involved in the Sect. 4.5—Architectural emergencies

Code	Name	Description	InD	Level	Class
B_EV	Elements of value	Presence of elements with historical and cultural value (portal, epigraph, decorations, friezes, …)	1	D	B/GA
B_HR	Historical relevance	Distinctive cultural, historical, and identity features	1	D	B/GA

Table 4.6 According to the Table 4.1, the system of data involved in the Sect. 4.6—Condition survey

Code	Name	Description	Ref	Level	Class
B_CC	Condition Class of Building	Presence of decays	2	D	B/GA
U_CC	Condition Class of Urban Element	Presence of decays	2	D	T/GA

These indicators are derived through the identification of specific semantic relationships and the quantification of simple descriptors associated with each sub-component.

Subsequently, the preservation levels of the individual elements are aggregated to form a unified assessment of the overall condition of the building. This results in the definition of the Global State of Conservation, formalised as the Secondary Indicator [B_CS]. With reference to the contents of Table 4.11, the table outlines the rules underlying the T-DSS for the definition of the primary indicator B_Ccd, which pertains to each specific type of decay. This indicator is defined through the matrix-based correlation of the descriptors B_S (Seriousness), B_In (Intensity), and B_Ex (Extension), which collectively contribute to the structured determination of the conservation state of the individual building component. Moreover, for determining the conservation state of a sub-component in cases where multiple types of decay are present, the UNI CEN/TS standard recommends the application of a grouping method, which enables the synthesis of heterogeneous degradation types into a consistent evaluative outcome. In such cases, the condition class of each defect is defined according to the criteria outlined in Table 4.11, taking into account the highest value associated with the extension descriptor, specifically (>70%).

For each type of decay [B_Td], the defect is evaluated in terms of aggregated extension [D], taking into account the corresponding condition class [B_Ccd]. A specific correction factor [Fc] is then applied to the actual extension value in order to obtain a weighted extension of the defect. This procedure is formalised in Table 4.12, Eqs. (4.1) and (4.2).

$$D_i = Fc_i^{*} Ad_i \left(i = 1 \ldots n\right) \tag{4.1}$$

where D_i = i-th aggregate extension of decay. Fc_i = i-th corrective factor assessed according to the class of condition of the i-th decay (Table 4.12). Ad_i = extension of the i-th decay, in percentage.

Table 4.7 According to the Table 4.1, the system of data involved in the Sect. 4.7—Qualification of decays

Code	Name	Description	Ref	Level	Class
B_Td	Type of decay	Identification of decays	2	D	B/GA
B_S	Seriousness	Severity of degradation	2	D	B/GA
B_In	Intensity	Level of decay	2	D	B/GA
B_Ex	Extension	Extension of the decay area	2	D	B/GA
D	Aggregate extension of decay	Aggregate extension of decay area	2	D	B/GA
Fc	Corrective factor	Corrective factor assessed according to the class of condition of the single decay	2	D	B/GA
Ad	Extension of decay	Extension of the i-th decay, in percentage	2	D	B/GA
Ccd	Condition for single decay	Class of condition for single decay	2	PI	B/GA
B_CSW	Conservative state of wall	Qualification of the conservative state of wall	2	PI	B/GA
B_CSR	Conservative state of roof	Qualification of the conservative state of roof	2	PI	B/GA
B_CSWi	Conservative state of windows	Qualification of the conservative state of windows	2	PI	B/GA
B_BT	Recurrent building type	Type of building identified as combination of recurrent characters	1	PI	B/GA
B_CS	Global conservation state of building	State of conservation of building, considering all the components	1/2	SI	B/GA
B_IC	Building intervention class	Class of required intervention (ordinary maintenance, static recovery, …)	1/2	SI	B/GA
B_IPr	Building intervention priority index	Prioritisation of intervention considering value range of building intervention class and building type	1	SI	B/GA
U_AT	Urban asset type	Typical urban element identified as combination of recurrent characters	1	PI	T/GA
U_CS	Conservative class of urban element	Surface decay and physical lacks in paving	3	PI	T/GA
U_IC	Urban intervention class	Class of required intervention (urban maintenance, regeneration)	1/2	SI	T/GA
U_IPr	Urban intervention priority index	Prioritisation of intervention considering the value range of intervention class and type of urban element	1/2	SI	T/GA

Thus, the total extension of the defected area (D_{tot}) results as the sum of the i-th aggregated extension of decays (D_i):

$$D_{tot} = \Sigma D_i \left(i = 1 \ldots n\right) \quad (4.2)$$

Finally, the primary indicator of the conservation state for each sub-component [B_CSx] is determined according to Eq. (4.3), and qualitatively described based on the aggregated condition class as defined in Table 4.13.

Table 4.8 List of primary (PI) and secondary indicators (SI) and codes of combined descriptors and indicators

Code	Name	Combined descriptors
B_BT	Recurrent building type	B_Typ; Cl; CP; Fct; Use; nFa; PW; WiA; Str; WT; RT
B_Ccd	Class of condition for single decay	B_Td; S; In; Ex
B_Di	Aggregate extension of decay	B_Ccd; Fc; Ad
B_DiW	Total aggregate extension of wall decay	B_Di
B_DiR	Total aggregate extension of roof decay	B_Di
B_DiWi	Total aggregate extension of windows decay	B_Di
B_CSW	Conservative state of wall	B_DiW; WA
B_CSR	Conservative state of roof	B_DiR; RArf
B_CSWi	Conservative state of windows	B_DiWi; WiA
B_CS	Global conservation state of building	B_CSW; CSR; CSWi
B_IC	Building intervention class	B_BT; CS
B_IPr	Building intervention priority index	B_ IC
U_AT	Urban asset type	U_Cl; Fct; Use; ST
U_CS	Conservative class of urban element	U_CC
U_IC	Urban intervention class	U_AT; CS
U_IPr	Urban intervention priority index	U_IC

Table 4.9 Qualitative classification of the state of preservation of physical entities according to EN 16096:2012

Conservation class B/U_CC	Symptoms
CC0	No symptoms
CC1	Lieve symptoms
CC2	Symptoms of medium intensity
CC3	Severe symptoms

Table 4.10 Relations between classes and priority of intervention to the values of global conservation state of urban element

<table>
<tr><th rowspan="2">U_CS</th><th rowspan="2">Condition</th><th colspan="2">U_IC</th><th rowspan="2">U_Ipr</th></tr>
<tr><th>U_AT with historical value</th><th>U_AT without historical value</th></tr>
<tr><td>0</td><td>Excellent</td><td rowspan="4">Urban restoration</td><td rowspan="2">Ordinary maintenance</td><td rowspan="2">2</td></tr>
<tr><td>1</td><td>Good</td></tr>
<tr><td>2</td><td>Fairly good</td><td rowspan="2">Urban renovation</td><td rowspan="2">1</td></tr>
<tr><td>3</td><td>Low</td></tr>
</table>

Table 4.11 Values of classes of conditions (Ccd) (1–6) as the combination of seriousness, intensity and extension descriptors

Seriousness	Intensity	Extension				
		Minimal (≤2%)	Inconsistent (>2%, ≤10%)	Consistent (>10%, ≤30%)	Significant (>30%, ≤70%)	Widespread (>70%)
Minor	Low	1	1	1	1	2
	Medium	1	1	1	2	3
	High	1	1	2	3	4
Serious	Low	1	1	1	2	3
	Medium	1	1	2	3	4
	High	1	2	3	4	5
Critical	Low	1	1	2	3	4
	Medium	1	2	3	4	5
	High	2	3	4	5	6

Table 4.12 Corrective factors for each class of conditions

Class of condition for single decay [Ccd]	Corrective factor [Fc]
1	1
2	1.02
3	1.10
4	1.30
5	1.70
6	2

$$B\_CS_x = D_{tot} / Ac \qquad (4.3)$$

where Ac = extension of sub-component, in percentage.

As far as the assessment of the secondary factor, the global conservation state of building [B_CS] is calculated as the result of the weighted average of decays and related sub-component extensions as described in Eq. (4.4):

$$B\_CS = \Sigma\left(CSW^{*}WA + CSR^{*}RA + CSW_i^{*}W_iA / WA + RA + W_iA\right) \qquad (4.4)$$

Table 4.13 Range of values of D_{tot}/Ac and associated values for the aggregated class of conditions

D_{tot}/Ac	Aggregated class of condition
$x \leq 1.01$	1
$1.01 < x \leq 1.04$	2
$1.04 < x \leq 1.15$	3
$1.15 < x \leq 1.40$	4
$1.40 < x \leq 1.78$	5
$x > 1.78$	6

Table 4.14 Relationship between intervention classes and priority levels in relation to the global conservation state of the building

		B_IC		
B_CS	Condition	Listed	Not listed	B_Ipr
1	Excellent	Building restoration	Ordinary maintenance	3
2	Good			
3	Fairly good		Extraordinary maintenance	2
4	Low			
5	Bad		Building renovation	1
6	Very Bad			

where B_CS = Global conservation state of building. B_CSW = Conservative state of walls. WA = Area of walls. B_CSR = Conservative state of roofs. B_RA = Area of roofs. CSW_i = Conservative state of windows. W_iA = Area of windows

With regard to the relationship between condition classes, intervention priorities, and the Global State of Conservation, the underlying rules are summarised in Table 4.14. Specifically:

- The classes of intervention are defined in accordance with the adopted preservation strategies. In line with conservation principles, distinctions are made not only based on the building's state of conservation but also in relation to any specific cultural or historical constraints. In cases involving buildings subject to direct heritage protection, conservative restoration represents the sole admissible class of intervention. Conversely, for broader historical urban fabrics, additional intervention classes—such as ordinary maintenance, extraordinary maintenance, and building rehabilitation—are recognised as appropriate responses, depending on the assessed Global Conservation State.
- The priority of intervention is introduced as an index representing the level of urgency associated with each intervention class. It is expressed as a numerical value ranging from 1 to 3, corresponding inversely to the seriousness of the required intervention—with lower numerical values indicate higher urgency.

Finally, the semantic data are encoded and structured for their proper integration with the CityGML standard. In particular, the data are mapped to the semantic structures already defined within the *Building* (B) and *Transportation* (T) modules of

CityGML standard. Where specific semantics are not natively conceptualised within the CityGML standard, they have been integrated using the *GenericAttribute* class. This approach extends the semantic digital model to support the characterisation of existing architectural heritage, emphasising both the potential and the multiscale capabilities of data processing. Accordingly, for each thematic section (Tables 4.1, 4.2, 4.3, 4.4, 4.5, 4.6, and 4.7) provide a detailed overview of the relevant parameters. Each table introduces the codification, name, description, and informational value of the parameters, structured according to thematic classifications. Additionally, the tables highlight the correspondence with the categories of Informational Dimensions and the associated CityGML *Class*.

4.3 The Conceptualisation of 3hD-DigitalCode (3D Historic District Digital Code)

This section presents the 3D Historic District Digital Code (3hD-DigitalCode), developed to enhance the technical understanding of historic districts. The 3hD-DigitalCode emerges from the integration of conventional Cultural Heritage recovery processes with the advanced capabilities of CityGML-based three-dimensional models. This integration is supported by spatial information systems, relational databases, decision support systems, and digital tools such as photogrammetry and Virtual Reality approaches.

To address the critical issues associated with traditional conservation practices, particularly the fragmentation and lack of integration of information across different phases, as well as the limited collaboration among professionals (engineers, architects, restorers), a comprehensive and structured digital code of practice has been developed.

The 3hD-DigitalCode provides a systematic framework that supports the entire conservation process. It aligns with the conventional phases of heritage conservation, namely: (1) technical knowledge, focused on historical, architectural, and material analysis, including the study of architectural-structural and functional transformations over time and the current state of conservation; (2) pre-diagnosis, involving the cataloguing and organisation of data acquired in the previous phase, with the objective of formulating preliminary hypotheses to inform the planning of subsequent diagnostic investigations; and (3) diagnosis, in which the collected information is further developed to define appropriate recovery strategies.

By adhering to these structured phases, the 3hD-DigitalCode seeks to streamline operationally the conservation workflow, promote interdisciplinary collaboration, and ensure a thorough understanding of the historical and architectural significance of the heritage asset.

The digital code of practice articulates technical knowledge across four interrelated levels:

1. Information Level. It defines the nature and typology of the data encoded within the system, offering a clear understanding of the information structure.
2. Thematic Level. It addresses various categories of historical heritage, with particular focus on the built environment, including both residential and special-purpose buildings, as well as urban elements such as squares, streets, and open spaces.
3. Disciplinary Level. It supports multiple fields of inquiry, contributing to structural, architectural, and historical analyses.
4. Definitional Level. It introduces a multi-scalar framework for heritage analysis. At the macro-scale, it qualifies aggregate-level data through geometric and spatial information, while at the micro-scale, it focuses on individual buildings and urban spaces through semantic and technical knowledge.

By structuring information along these four levels, the 3hD-DigitalCode enhances technical understanding and promotes a holistic approach to heritage analysis and conservation—especially in relation to the architectural and urban assets.

Specifically, the main phases comprising the 3hD-DigitalCode are shown in Fig. 4.2 and outlined below.

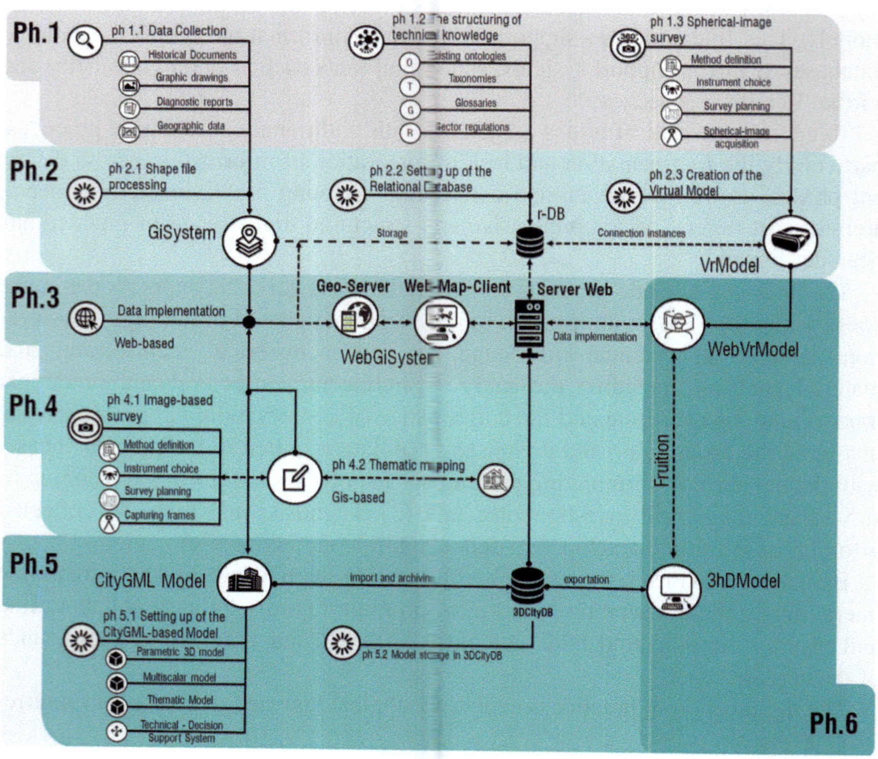

Fig. 4.2 Phases and sub-phases involved in the 3hD-DigitalCode

4.3.1 Ph. 1 Knowledge Analysis

The first phase focuses on the acquisition of both quantitative and qualitative data, which are essential for the analysis and interpretation of the area under investigation.

This phase is conducted across two scales of analysis: the micro-scale, addressing individual architectural buildings, and the macro-scale, concerning broader urban aggregates and specific urban entities considered as integrated systems.

Here, three sub-phases are required:

4.3.1.1 ph 1.1. Data Collection

The cognitive process consists of a preliminary sub-phase.

At the macro-scale, it requires:

1. Historical-documentary and archival research aimed at analysing the diachronic evolution of architectural artefacts and the associated urban transformations.
2. Morpho-typological and architectural analysis of the urban fabric, undertaken to identify building types (e.g. terraced houses, tower houses) and urban types (e.g. streets, squares, open spaces).
3. Site morphology analysis, focused on understanding the orographic and morphological configuration of the terrain and extracting planimetric and altimetric data.
4. Identification of primary urban infrastructure systems, including the presence of water supply, sewage networks, electricity, and gas distribution.

In addition, this phase involves the analysis and acquisition of territorial-scale data (orthophotos, regional technical maps, and digital terrain/surface models). These datasets are essential for the subsequent georeferencing of architectural elements (ph_2.1) and the elaboration of three-dimensional models of individual buildings (ph_5.1).

At the micro-scale, the investigation is focused on the intrinsic characteristics of individual artefacts, including:

1. Identification of construction techniques, such as load-bearing masonry or mixed systems.
2. Characterisation of materials used in structural and non-structural components (walls and roofs).
3. Assessment of the conservation state of architectural elements.
4. Survey of technological systems installed in the building (water, sewage, electrical, and thermal systems).
5. Analysis of historical and current building uses.

Specifically, the information collected during this phase and its sub-phases is derived from comprehensive bibliographic, archival, and documentary research.

This process involves the systematic collection and cataloguing of data preserved by both public and private institutions, including state archives, libraries, and professional offices. Such thorough data acquisition aims to provide an in-depth understanding of the site's evolutionary history, morphological characteristics, and material-constructive features. The objective is to acquire an extensive and detailed understanding of the site's historical development, morphological features, and material-constructive properties.

4.3.1.2 ph 1.2. The Structuring of Technical Knowledge

This sub-phase focuses on the encoding and organisation of the extensive body of collected information to ensure its proper storage and management, in alignment with the conceptual model defined in Sect. 4.2. The model is structured as a logical-relational schema integrating multiple knowledge sources, including taxonomies from glossaries on stone deterioration patterns, existing ontologies for the spatial and semantic representation of Cultural Heritage, regulatory frameworks related to the assessment of conservation states in building systems, and well-established disciplinary methodologies. Specifically, three categories of parameters—described in Sect. 4.2 and detailed in Tables 4.1, 4.2, 4.3, 4.4, 4.5, 4.6, and 4.7—were identified.

As previously mentioned, the logical and mathematical relationships underpinning the ontological structure are intended to support a Technical Decision Support System (T-DSS). Moreover, the ontology-based structuring also enables the qualification of historic heritage at varying levels of granularity, thereby supporting the informed definition of conservation and intervention strategies.

4.3.1.3 ph. 1.3. Spherical-Image Survey

The area under investigation is digitally surveyed through a rapid acquisition using a spherical image-based approach. This sub-phase begins with the definition of a survey plan, which serves as a preparatory step for the digitalisation of the built environment. Based on the previously collected technical data, expert users are required to plan the photographic acquisition procedures. The process starts with the design of an image acquisition strategy using a spherical camera head. This includes determining the number and positioning of the capture points, guided by knowledge of the morphological characteristics of the urban context. This step is crucial to ensure both optimal overlap between spherical images and maximum coverage of the built environment. Two operational ways may be adopted for image acquisition: (1) manual deployment using tripods, or (2) automated methods using robotic platforms or Unmanned Aerial Vehicles (UAVs). Following this, the actual spherical image-based survey is conducted, constituting the operative phase of the digital acquisition process. The capture of spherical RGB images (Sph_RGB) in the real environment is carried out in accordance with the predefined acquisition strategy and planning parameters.

4.3.2 Ph 2. Creation of Systems and Digital Models

The second phase involves the development of both the geographical and relational information system and the virtual model. This phase is articulated into three interrelated sub-phases:

4.3.2.1 ph 2.1. Shape File Processing

Each architectural entity, along with its associated geometric properties, is accurately geolocated within the designated reference system. In particular, the shapefile is processed using available territorial datasets (e.g. regional technical maps, digital surface models and digital terrain models) to enable the spatial representation of urban fabrics. The resulting Geographical Information System (GiSystem) is then integrated with a relational Database (r-DB), allowing for the correlation between spatial and semantic-technical data.

4.3.2.2 ph 2.2. Setting Up of the Relational Database (r-DB)

The r-DB is structured to allow the filling and systematisation of semantic data required for the goal (descriptors in Tables 4.1, 4.2, 4.3, 4.4, 4.5, 4.6, and 4.7), resulting from the initial data collection. The r-DB structure adheres to the conceptual schema defined in Phase 1.2. To this end, the informative and relational database is implemented using PostgreSQL, with PostGIS as the spatial extension, and managed through the pgAdmin interface. Given the multidisciplinary nature of the data (historical, architectural, and diagnostic domains) and the heterogeneity of formats (e.g. drawings, images, documents), all information must be appropriately encoded using alphanumeric values. This ensures consistent integration and querying across domains. The r-DB is tightly integrated with the GiSystem, enabling detailed relational correlations between datasets. Each architectural entity is associated with a unique identifier (ID), which serves as the primary key for establishing one-to-many relationships among various data entries. Consequently, all data are linked to both the corresponding vector polygon representing the architectural entity in the GiSystem (ph 2.1) and to the corresponding hotspot in the Virtual Model (VrModel, ph 2.3), ensuring a coherent connection between semantic, spatial, and visual representations.

4.3.2.3 ph 2.3. Creation of the Virtual Model (VrModel)

The Virtual Model (VrModel) represents the digitalisation phase of the historic district through a process referred to as spherical joining. Specifically, VrModels are structured as Virtual Tours based on spherical images, which are logically interconnected and enriched with multiple layers of information. These models serve to generate realistic digital replicas of architectural structures and urban entities, while supporting their technical interpretation in accordance with the required levels of knowledge.

Each VrModel constitutes a unique digital representation within a Virtual Environment (VE), enhanced by structured, information-rich content (Fig. 4.3). The VE is generated from the spatial organisation of the spherical panoramas collected in Phase 1.3, arranged according to the predefined acquisition plan.

Furthermore, each VrModel is linked to a relational database (r-DB), which stores and encodes the associated information according to defined semantic levels. This database structure supports advanced conservation analysis, particularly in Phase 4. Within each VE, specific hotspots are positioned at key architectural elements or urban entities. These hotspots are labelled using a unique identifier (ID) that links them directly to the corresponding records in the r-DB.

In this way, the VrModel and r-DB together function as a technical support tool, facilitating structured access to the information collected and encoded in compliance with the schema established in Phase 1.2.

This integrated system—comprising the GiSystem, the relational database (r-DB), and the VrModel—is designed to feed into the subsequent phase (Phase 3), which focuses on historical heritage interpretation via web-based integration within a unified digital platform. At the core of this system is the WebGiSystem, which incorporates the WebVrModel. The entire platform is accessible online via GeoServer, supported by a Web Map Client and hosted on a dedicated web-server.

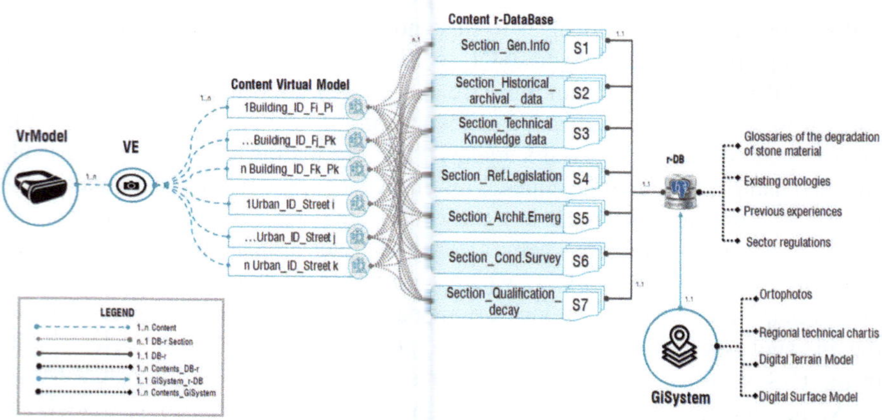

Fig. 4.3 Conceptual structure for connecting the VR Model with the GiSystem through the r-DB

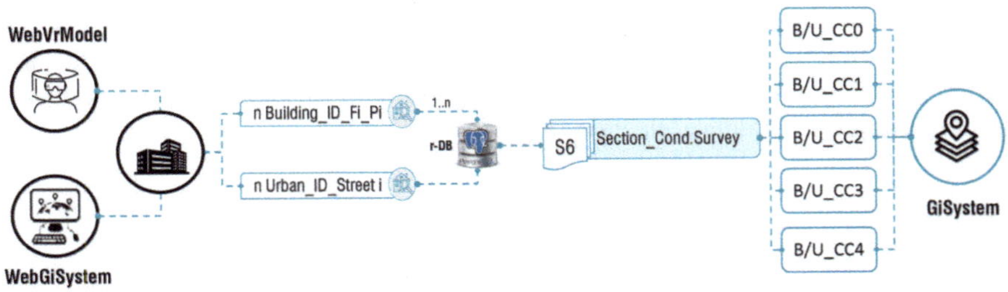

Fig. 4.4 Conceptual structure for implementing the data in r-DB and GiSystem via web

4.3.3 *Ph 3. Qualitative Surveys In Situ and/or On-Desk*

The third phase involves the qualitative analysis of the urban and built environments within the historic district, conducted by qualified technical experts (e.g. professional technicians). The operational workflow varies depending on the mode of inspection, which can be carried out in two types of survey: (a) on-site, using portable digital devices such as tablets; or (b) remotely, through desktop-based applications.

Accordingly, the implementation and updating of the information system can follow two approaches: (1) on-site data entry, where expert users input data directly into the relational database (r-DB) during field inspections; or (2) remote data entry, in which technical evaluations are performed via visual inspection using the integrated WebGiSystem and WebVrModel platforms (Fig. 4.4).

4.3.4 *Ph 4. Quantitative Analysis of the State of Preservation on a Building Scale*

The fourth phase concerns the quantitative analysis of the state of preservation at the building scale. According to the T-DSS (Sect. 4.1), only for buildings classified as having a low condition class, qualitatively assessed by the technical expert during the in situ/on-desk survey (Phase 3), is a second level of analysis required.

In detail, two sub-phases are required:

4.3.4.1 ph 4.1—Image-Based Survey

This sub-phase involves the Close Range Photogrammetry acquisition, based on SfM (Structure from Motion) procedures, aimed at producing RGB point clouds (RGBCloud) and, where applicable, textured polygonal meshes and orthophotos.

The elaboration of the RGBCloud is guided by a preliminary analysis of the built heritage (ph 1.1), which supports the definition of the survey type (aerial and/or terrestrial) and the planning of the photogrammetric acquisition. Subsequently, the images captured on-site are pre-processed using photo-editing software, with the aim of reducing or eliminating visual noise resulting from suboptimal environmental conditions during data collection (e.g. poor lighting).

4.3.4.2 ph 4.2—Thematic Mapping for Conservation Assessment

Aimed at qualifying the main building components (such as walls, roofs, and windows), this sub-phase focuses on the identification and classification of decay types and their corresponding qualitative and quantitative indicators (Table 4.7).

Each digitised architectural entity is imported into the GIS environment and assigned a unique identification code (ID), ensuring consistent referencing and traceability. Here, the types of decay (B_Td) are classified in accordance with the ICOMOS-ISCS Glossary, while the associated parameters—Seriousness (B_S), Intensity (B_In), and Extension (B_Ex)—are assigned by qualified professionals for each identified form of deterioration (Fig. 4.5). The corresponding levels of detail for the selected indicators are then associated with each architectural unit (vector polygon), and this information is systematically recorded, encoded, and integrated within both the GiSystem and the associated relational database (r-DB), as sub-properties linked to the respective ID.

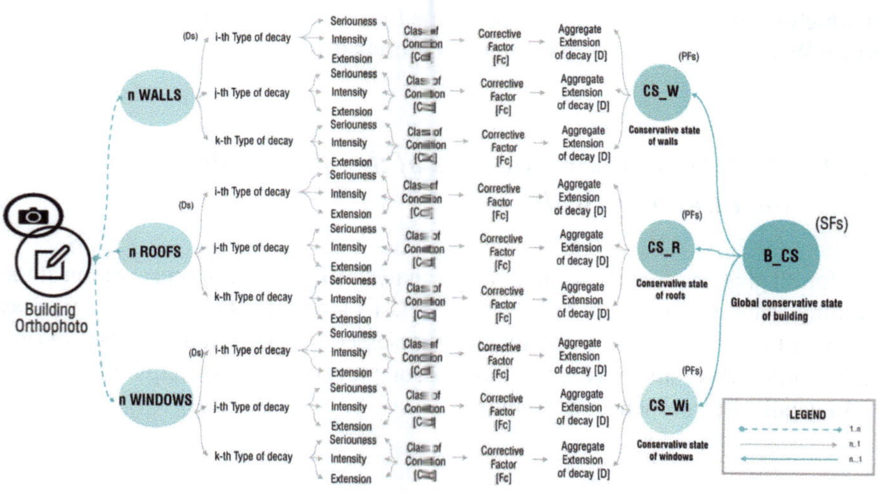

Fig. 4.5 Conceptual structure of the evaluation of the conservative state of building components according to the T-DSS rules

4.3.5 Ph 5. Implementation of the Parametric Model According to the CityGML Standard

The fifth phase focuses on the development of the urban parametric model in compliance with the CityGML standard. This process is divided into three sub-phases:

4.3.5.1 ph 5.1 Setting Up of the CityGML-Based Model

This sub-phase focuses on the development of the parametric model, drawing upon the geometric and geolocated data contained in the shape file (ph 2.1), the general semantic information structured in the ph.2.2, and the features derived from the mapping process in ph 4.2. All data collected within the GiSystem (.shp files) and r-DB, including both geometric and semantic features, are translated into the CityGML standard format (.gml files) using the FME (Feature Manipulation Engine) visual programming environment. FME, a Spatial ETL (Extract, Transform, Load) tool, is designed to support the conversion of both spatial and semantic data in accordance with the CityGML standard. The process follows a dedicated ETL workflow within FME to establish both vertical relationships—linking individual city objects to their attributes—and horizontal relationships—connecting them to one another (Fig. 4.6).

In detail, the specific workbenches of the FME visual platform employed for this purpose are described as follows:

- Importing and reading of the .shp files for the model of the built and urban environment, in which the attributes were identified as catalogued in the GIS environment, and the raster file for the digital terrain model (*transformer: Read*).
- Processing of the digital terrain model (TIN), through the transformation of the raster data into an irregular triangular mesh, consequently transformed according to the CityGML standard, to enable the superimposition of further geometric-thematic models (*transformer: TINGenerator*).
- Creation of the geometric model (LOD1) of the built and urban environment, obtained by draping the previously elaborated ground surface and extruding the footprint area of buildings, streets, squares, and open spaces according to their heights. The realisation of the geometric model in LOD1 was carried out by extruding the collected heights included in the relative DSM, as well as the projections of the floors of each building, starting from the technical information reported in the starting .shp file (*transformer: SurfaceDraper and Extruder*).
- Codification of buildings using cadastral information, and streets, squares, and open spaces using toponymic data. All the buildings and urban entity are associated to a specific alphanumeric ID that includes data according to specific codes, with the aim of supporting the final search activities and visualisation of objects and data (*transformer: UUIDGenerator and String Concatenator*).

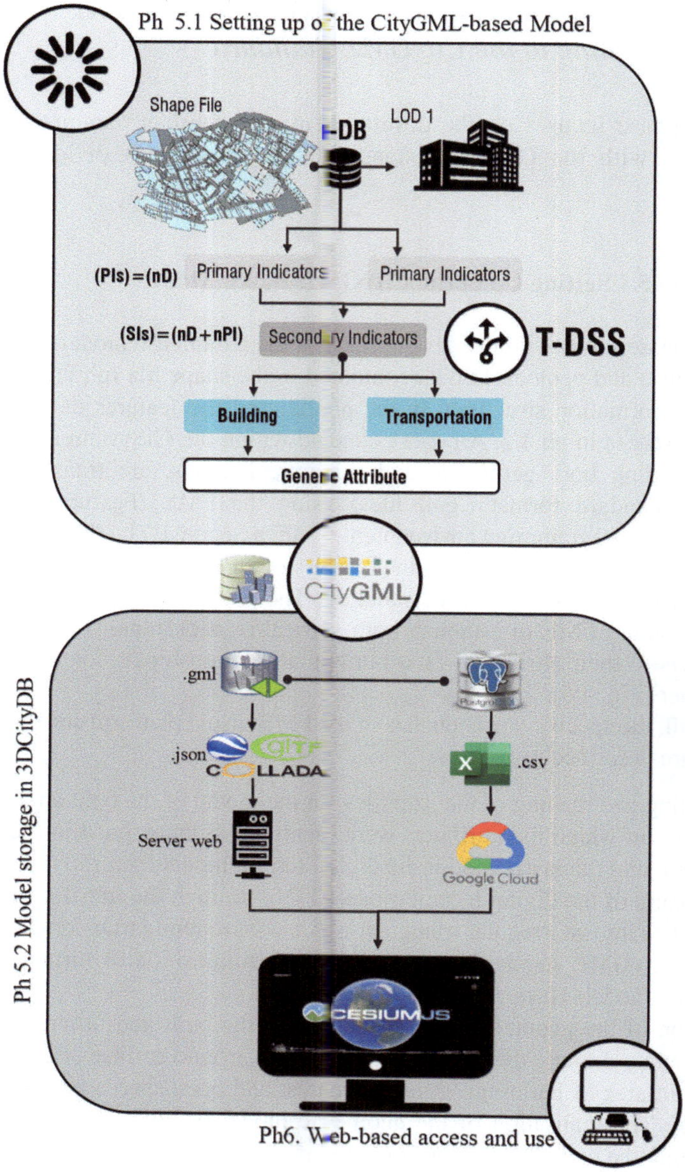

Fig. 4.6 Conceptual structure relating to the phases and tools for the development of the parametric model CityGML-based

- Implementation of the T-DSS by structuring logical relationships in accordance with the outlined rules. Here, the logical-relational structure is defined according to the T-DSS (Sect. 4.2). So, specific classes of attributes are set up according to the standard in order to introduce primary and secondary indicators related to the conservation levels of sub-components and buildings (U_CS, B_CSW, B_CSR, B_CSWi, B_CS), as well as the secondary indicators associated to the classes and priority of intervention of each building (U_IC, U_IPr, B_IC, B_Ipr). In parallel, CityGML attributes are generated, with all .shp features are translated in the CityGML standard through the creation of specific attributes that integrate the results of the T-DSS flow, with the implemented data (*script: AttributeCreator*).
- Establishing the connections between geometric entities—such as buildings, streets, squares, and open spaces—and their associated attributes, in order to characterise their nature and functional role of each geometric element (*CityGML LOD Name: Lod1MultiSurface; FeatureRole: cityObjectMember) (transformer: CityGMLGeometrySetter*).
- Development of a CityGML model aligned with thematic classes. In this workbench, all data are associated with the *Building* and *Transportation* classes when already structured according to the CityGML standard, or alternatively mapped through *_genericAttribute* and *ExternalReferences* as a final step of semantic enhancement. In particular, an *ExternalReference* establishes a hyperlink from a *_CityObject* to a corresponding element in an external information system. Each reference specifies the name of the external system—identified by a URI—and the identifier of the external object, provided either as a string or a URI.

At this stage, the results of scientific and technical analyses conducted on the district converge to address three fundamental aspects: (1) the structured management of semantic data derived from external computations, which represents a key element; (2) the detailed examination of building characteristics through site surveys and external measurements, undertaken with critical rigour; and (3) the incorporation of the legal context related to the protection of the historic ensemble, considered essential.

Simultaneously, both admissible intervention strategies and their execution priorities are stored in the 3D database as attributes associated with the corresponding buildings. These provide valuable support for professionals and technical expertise involved in the process.

4.3.5.2 ph 5.2 Model Storage in 3DCityDB

The parametric model is incorporated into the 3D City Database (3DCityDB) for the archival and administration of CityGML data (Fig. 4.6). The CityGML-based model is imported in the 3DCityBD, a CityGML-based geographic informative system designed for the analysis and management of data within the parametric 3D model, and integrated with a relational database implemented in PostgreSQL/PostGIS, accessible via the PgAdmin graphical interface. The process requires a medium-to-high level of IT expertise due to the programming involved. In this phase, the database is also prepared for the management of data by end-users (administrative and technical). Accordingly, .csv files can be generated from the database and shared with controlled access levels through the Google Cloud Platform via the Google Sheets API. This facilitates ongoing management of the parametric model, allowing sector-specific users to interact with it over time in accordance with established usage protocols. Furthermore, the system enables the export of semantic-thematic and geometric-topological data for web-based visualisation. This requires the data to be restructured and refined to ensure clarity and accessibility within the online environment.

4.3.6 Ph 6. Elaboration of the Model for Technical Use

The sixth phase involves the use of the CityGMLModel and the VrModel via a web-based approach, enabling their integration into a platform specifically designed to host both models (Fig. 4.6). This phase concerns the visualisation and interaction of the 3D CityGML-based model through the 3DCityDB Web Map Client. During this phase, all end-users can interact with the model and access semantic information at the building scale through a user-friendly web browser interface. The phase is designed to facilitate straightforward access to classification data and intervention priorities at the district level for all stakeholders involved in building preservation activities. The model supports queries for cadastral data of buildings, with associated semantic information displayed in dedicated pop-up windows. The visualisation process for authorised users requires the import of both the .json file and the associated sheets from the preceding phase. While Google Sheets enables the visualisation of thematic data, only administrative users have the permission to modify and manage the content. Simultaneously, a connection to the WebVrModel is allowed from the pop-windows, enhancing the perception of the investigated environment, although in this instance the hotspots of the virtual model are limited to the visualisation of the data.

4.4 Remarks on the Developed Methodology

The described 3hD-DigitalCode approach is conceived as an integrated and adaptive framework designed to support the recovery and management of historic districts. It is characterised by three fundamental dimensions: (1) multi-scalar, as it incorporates geometric data and contextual information across different spatial and temporal levels of analysis; (2) multidisciplinary, as it integrates heterogeneous data sources—ranging from information technologies to thematic and semantic datasets—thereby bridging architectural, urban, and regulatory knowledge domains; and (3) multi-user, as it is structured to address the specific needs of a broad spectrum of stakeholders, including administrative bodies, technical experts, and professional practitioners. By embracing this multi-faceted configuration, the 3hD-DigitalCode recognises the inherent complexity of conservation processes, promoting adaptability and interoperability. This ensures that the digital code not only aligns with traditional conservation principles but also enhances decision-making processes, fostering collaborative and well-informed interventions across different operational contexts.

To support and demonstrate its potentialities, the digital code of practice is ultimately applied and validated through two emblematic pilot cases, selected to reflect the intrinsic criticalities associated with both physical degradation and regulatory obsolescence affecting the identified historic areas. The outcomes of this application, together with a critical discussion on the validation process and its implications for future conservation practices, are thoroughly examined in Chap. 5, where the operational performance and potential of the developed digital code are extensively analysed.

References

1. Lasorella M, Cantatore E (2023) 3Dcitymodels to support technical knowledge and management of historic built environments. A semantic CityGML-based model for the ancient core of Carovigno (BR), Italy. SCIRES-IT-SCIentific Res Inf Technol 13:101–116
2. Lasorella M, Cantatore E (2023) 3D models CityGML-based combined with technical decision support system for the setting up of digital conservation plans of historic districts. Int Arch Photogramm Remote Sens Spat Inf Sci XLVIII-M–2:911–918. https://doi.org/10.5194/isprs-archives-XLVIII-M-2-2023-911-2023
3. Wijesuriya G, Thompson J, Young C (2013) Managing cultural world heritage. UNESCO
4. ICOMOS (2003) Principles for the analysis, conservation and structural restoration of architectural heritage
5. Vergès-Belmin V (2008) Illustrated glossary on stone deterioration patterns. ICOMOS
6. Doerr M (2003) The CIDOC conceptual reference module: an ontological approach to semantic interoperability of metadata. AI Mag 24:75
7. Noardo F (2018) Architectural heritage semantic 3D documentation in multi-scale standard maps. J Cult Herit 32:156–165. https://doi.org/10.1016/j.culher.2018.02.009
8. Yaagoubi R, Al-Gilani A, Baik A et al (2019) SEH-SDB: a semantically enriched historical spatial database for documentation and preservation of monumental heritage based on CityGML. Appl Geomat 11:53–68. https://doi.org/10.1007/s12518-018-0238-y

Chapter 5
Application and Validation of 3hD-DigitalCode to Pilot Cases

Abstract The Digital Code of Practice elaborated in this book is applied and validated for the management of the existing architectural heritage through VR-based rapid approaches, as well as through the use of a multiscale and multidisciplinary digital information system for the analysis, modelling and cataloguing of real cases. Specifically, the Digital Code of Practice is tested and validated on two emblematic pilot cases with respect to the intrinsic criticalities related to the physical and regulatory obsolescence of buildings (lack of maintenance activities and/or rehabilitation interventions).

Keywords Testing · CityGML · Historic district · El Cabanyal-Canyamelar Valencia · Carovigno

As outlined in the previous chapters, the recovery and management of historic districts require a comprehensive approach that integrates multidisciplinary expertise and multiscale analyses. This complexity calls for methodologies capable of simultaneously addressing both the intrinsic factors, such as morpho-typologies, construction techniques, and architectural significance, and the extrinsic factors, including historical transformations, social and cultural values. The 3hD-DigitalCode, conceived as a conceptual and operational framework, addresses this need by enabling the identification, assessment, and integration of these factors with respect to regulatory compliance and their contribution to local identity.

This chapter applies and validates the 3hD-DigitalCode through two emblematic pilot cases:

1. The historical area of El Cabanyal-Canyamelar, located in the Poblats Marítims district of Valencia (Spain), chosen for its distinctive morpho-typological and architectural evolution. Beyond its physical and typological richness, El Cabanyal-Canyamelar represents a paradigmatic case of the conflicts between urban development pressures and heritage conservation. Most notably, the Urban Regeneration Plan for the Historic Area (*Plan Especial de Protección y Reforma*

M. Lasorella et al., *Architectural Heritage Management via Digital Code of Practice*, SpringerBriefs in Architectural Design and Technology,
https://doi.org/10.1007/978-981-95-5106-4_5

Integral del Cabanyal-Canyamelar—PEPRI 2001) posed a significant threat to the neighbourhood's historical fabric, sparking widespread protests and intense debates over its cultural and architectural identity. This situation highlights the vulnerability of historic districts to planning decisions that prioritise redevelopment over preservation.
2. The historic district of Carovigno, a small town in the province of Brindisi (Italy), selected for its diverse historical and architectural features that reflect the stratification of its urban fabric. Conversely, these features have prompted various urban regeneration activities aimed at enhancing and adjusting existing urbanisation services. However, these efforts have resulted in thematic archival and documentary analyses that are not sufficiently consolidated within a comprehensive Recovery Plan. This has given rise to a complex system of historical and technical information, encompassing original characteristics, uncontrolled and controlled transformations, and the current state of structures, necessitating a comprehensive reorganisation.

Moreover, given the large amount of data required to create the database and generate results, for the historical area of El Cabanyal-Canyamelar (Valencia, Spain) it was considered useful to apply Phases 1-2-3-4 of the digital code of practice to a specific study area to validate the acquisition of technical knowledge information remotely using Virtual Reality techniques. In contrast, for the historic district of Carovigno (Brindisi, Italy), the complete workflow of the digital code of practice has been implemented and validated (Fig. 5.1).

Through these pilot cases, the chapter demonstrates the implementation and validation of decision support information systems based on the elaborated relational-logical structure. Furthermore, it explores the development of streamlined systems for the acquisition and analysis of architectural built heritage using Virtual Reality techniques, as well as the application of a CityGML-based model. This model not only supports the dissemination of knowledge among all stakeholders throughout the process, but also fosters interoperability between institutional-scientific entities and public administrations. Ultimately, the proposed approach contributes to the planning and design of recovery interventions at the urban scale, addressing critical issues associated with physical degradation and functional obsolescence in historic districts. Within this framework, digital systems and models leverage the capabilities of ontologies—whose rules and relationships are explicitly defined—to ensure consistent and interoperable information flows during the cataloguing, archiving, and systematisation of conservation and maintenance activities.

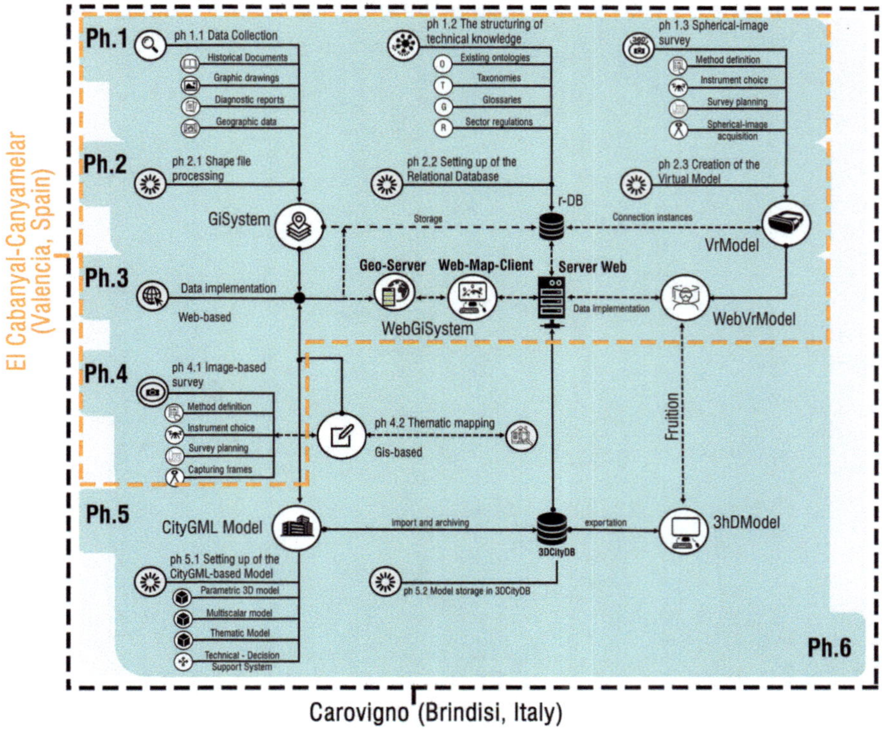

Fig. 5.1 Phases of the digital code of practice applied and validated for the pilot case of the historic neighbourhood of El Cabanyal-Canyamelar (Spain). In light blue the phases applied

5.1 Pilot Case 1—El Cabanyal-Canyamelar Valencia (Spain)

As introduced in the previous section, specific phases of the 3hD-DigitalCode have been implemented in a historic area of Valencia's El Cabanyal-Canyamelar neighbourhood located in the *Poblats Marítims* district of Valencia (Spain) (Fig. 5.2). The selection of the study area was specifically determined through a preliminary documentary-archival knowledge analysis. This analysis facilitated the identification of a historical area, urbanistically encompassed into the Cabanyal-Canyamelar Special Plan (*Plan Especial del Cabanyal-Canyamelar y su entorno urbano- PEC*), falling under the protection regime of the Property of Cultural Interest (*BIC-CH Original core of the El Cabanyal-Canyamelar expansion*) (Fig. 5.3), and part of the protected historic complex Cabanyal-Canyamelar-Cap de França according to current planning (Fig. 5.4). Within this area, most buildings (1) date back to pre-1936 (Fig. 5.5) as their construction period, (2) were in a state of low preservation in 2013 (Fig. 5.6), and (3) are privately owned (Fig. 5.7).

The earliest historical records of maritime settlements in the city of Valencia (Spain) date back to the thirteenth century and the conquest of the city by Jaume

Fig. 5.2 Location of Valencia in Spain (above) and spatial delimitation of the historical area studied of El Cabanyal-Canyamelar neighbourhood (under), with background map data © OpenStreetMap contributors, available under the Open Database License (ODbL)

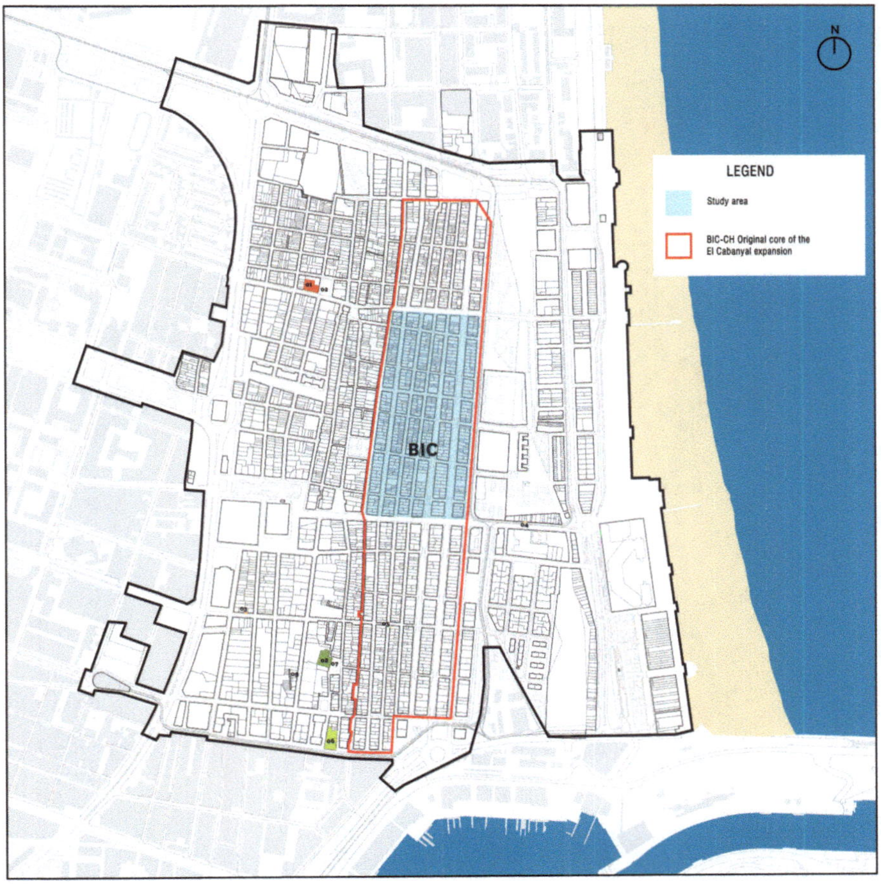

Fig. 5.3 The technical document of the Cabanyal-Canyamelar Special Plan showing the perimeter of the BIC-CH core of the El Cabanyal-Canyamelar expansion and the study area (image created starting from details available on the Valencia City Council website. Link Document (pg. 19) [1])

I. Although there is evidence of scattered fishermen's huts, used by those who worked both in the sea and in the Albufera lake (as mentioned in the *Chronicle of Jaume I*), the king rewarded 500 sailors, some of whom were located in what is now El Grao (close to the study area), for their support during the campaign by granting them the right to use the land while maintaining royal ownership in exchange for a tribute. This led to the emergence of a new settlement, which was officially recognised in 1249 as Vila Nova Maris Valentiae (*Villanueva del Mar*), endowed with its own administrative and judicial bodies. Throughout the thirteenth, fourteenth, and fifteenth centuries, the town experienced significant maritime and commercial growth, enhancing its importance as a strategic maritime location. Consequently, it was progressively fortified to withstand attacks from pirates and privateers.

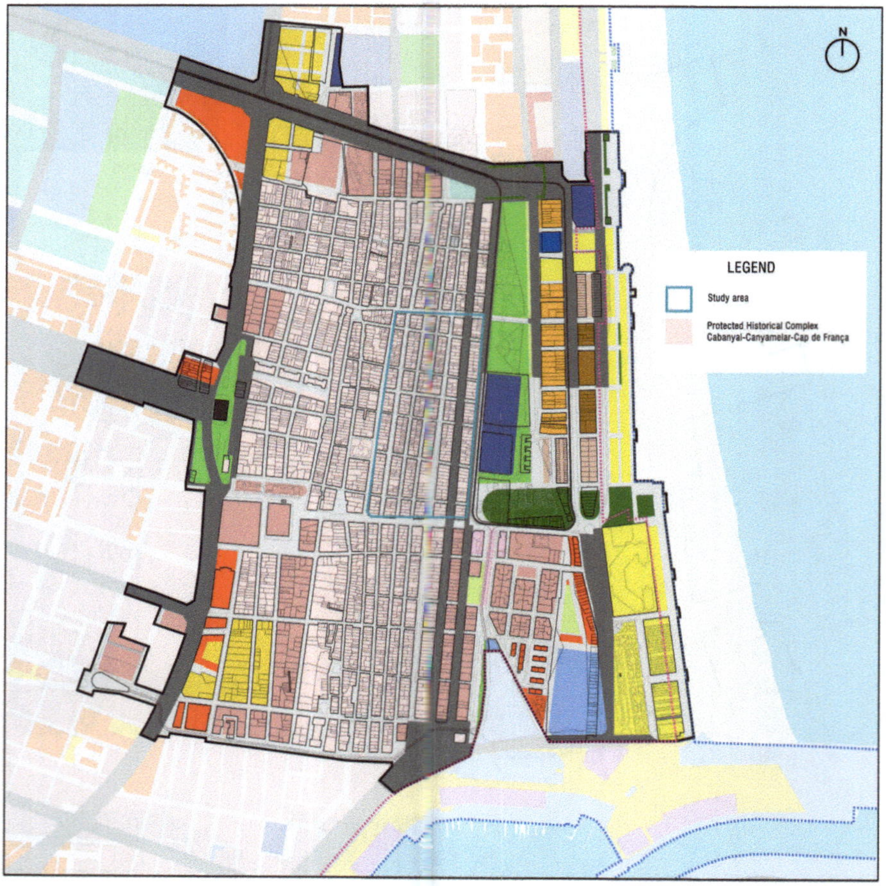

Fig. 5.4 The technical document of the Cabanyal-Canyamelar Special Plan showing the area of the Protected Historical Complex Cabanyal-Canyamelar-Cap de França and the study area (image created starting from details available on the Valencia City Council website. Link Document (pg. 24) [1])

During this period, a sandy strip north of the village walls extended, separating the land from the sea. In the eighteenth century, inhabitants began to settle informally on these lands, which were originally part of the *Real Patrimonio* acquired by right of conquest. Towards the end of the eighteenth century, informal settlements were consolidated, giving shape to the El Cabanyal-Canyamelar district as a distinctive maritime village.

Throughout the nineteenth century, El Cabanyal-Canyamelar experienced continued growth and development, evolving into a significant centre for fishermen and the local community. This expansion faced an initial obstacle with the construction of the railway network. The barriers to the east of the historic quarter initially impeded urban growth, restricting the expansion of the urban grid. However, once

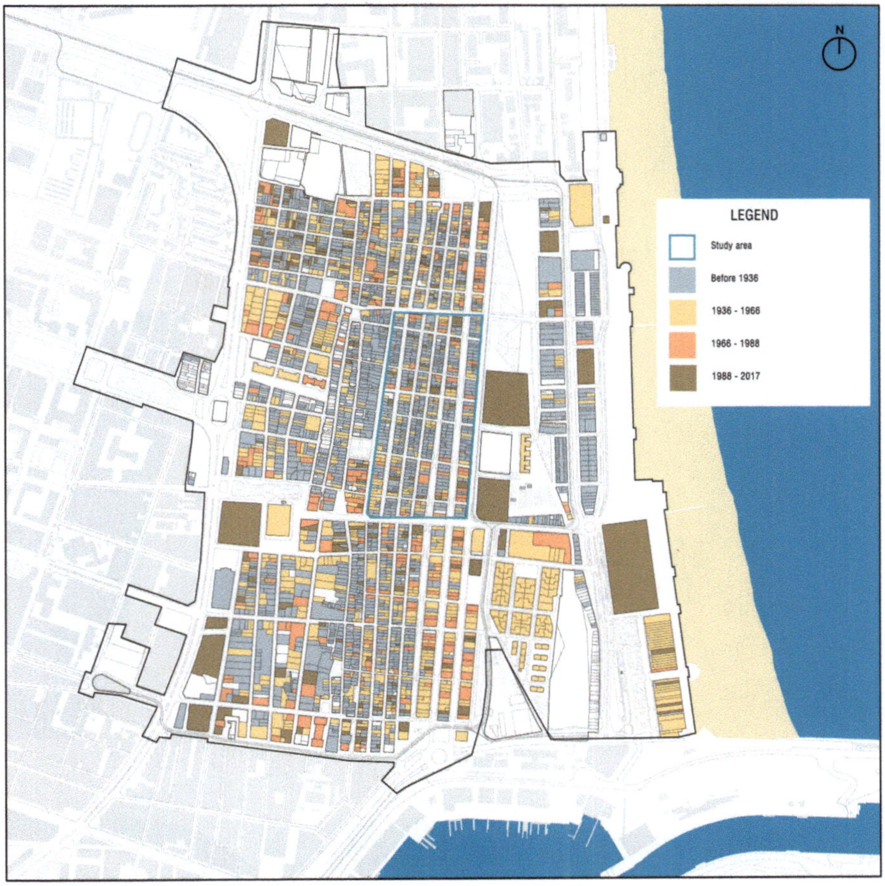

Fig. 5.5 The technical document of the Cabanyal-Canyamelar Special Plan showing the construction period of the buildings and the study area (image created starting from details available on the Valencia City Council website. Link Document (pg. 12) [1])

these barriers were overcome, thanks to a new retreat of the coastline, a second noteworthy expansion of the urban fabric unfolded [2].

Simultaneously, increasing demographic pressure served as a catalyst for urban development, prompting a redefinition of the urban grid. This marked the beginning of a phase of suburban colonisation to the west of the historic district. The urban grid gradually expanded its boundaries, initially progressing westwards and subsequently reaching, and even surpassing the railway routes to the north.

This shift in the direction of growth has not only addressed demographic needs but has also played a vital role in transforming and enhancing the overall urban structure of the district. Moreover, this dynamic adaptation of the urban grid demonstrated resilience and the capacity to evolve in response to changing community

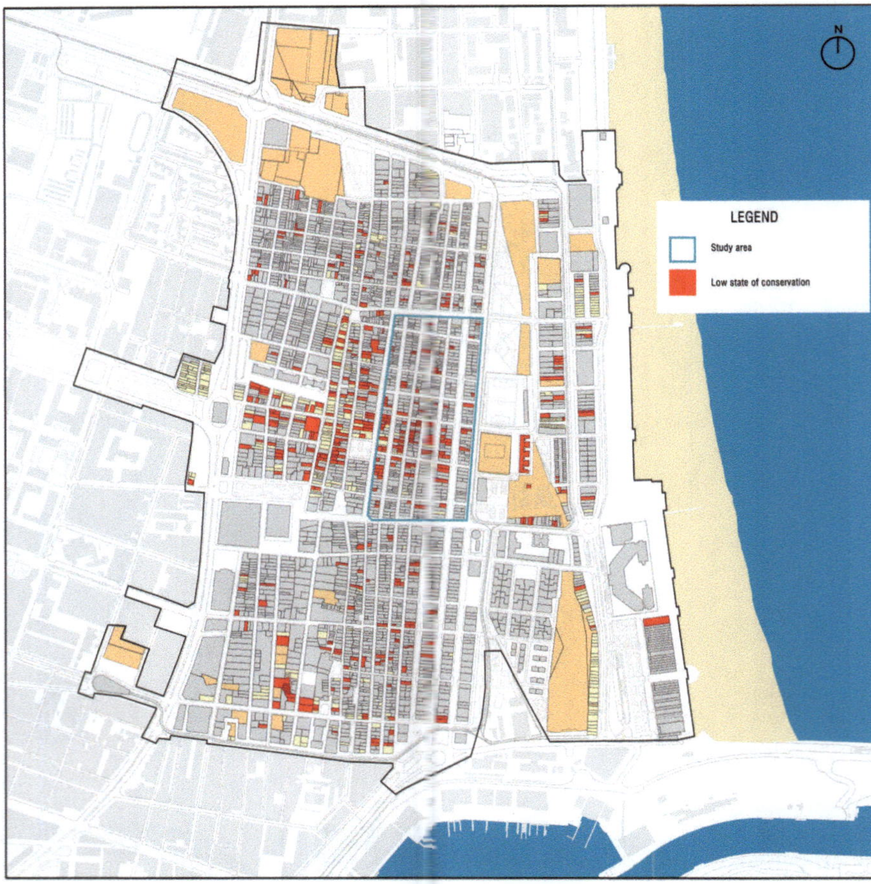

Fig. 5.6 The technical document of the Cabanyal-Canyamelar Special Plan highlights the low state of conservation of the buildings and the study area (image created starting from details available on the Valencia City Council website. Link Document (pg. 13) [1])

needs and urban dynamics. The expansion beyond the railway tracks towards the north represents a significant milestone in the village's growth.

Analysing Fig. 5.8, the Geometrical Plan of 1796 is a technical document that provides a detailed analysis of the state of construction in the original core of Valencia's historic neighbourhood, El Cabanyal-Canyamelar. This map reflects the urban configuration of the time with great accuracy.

By further analysing the 1796 Topographic Plan and its superimposition onto a 2023 photomap, the PEC drafting team confirms that the urban layout depicted in this plan is the origin of what is today known as the Old Town of El Cabanyal-Canyamelar, revealing with high precision a correspondence between the alignments drawn in 1796 and certain current streets [4]. The distinctive grid, derived from the previous alignments of the old barracas, extends from the beach to the

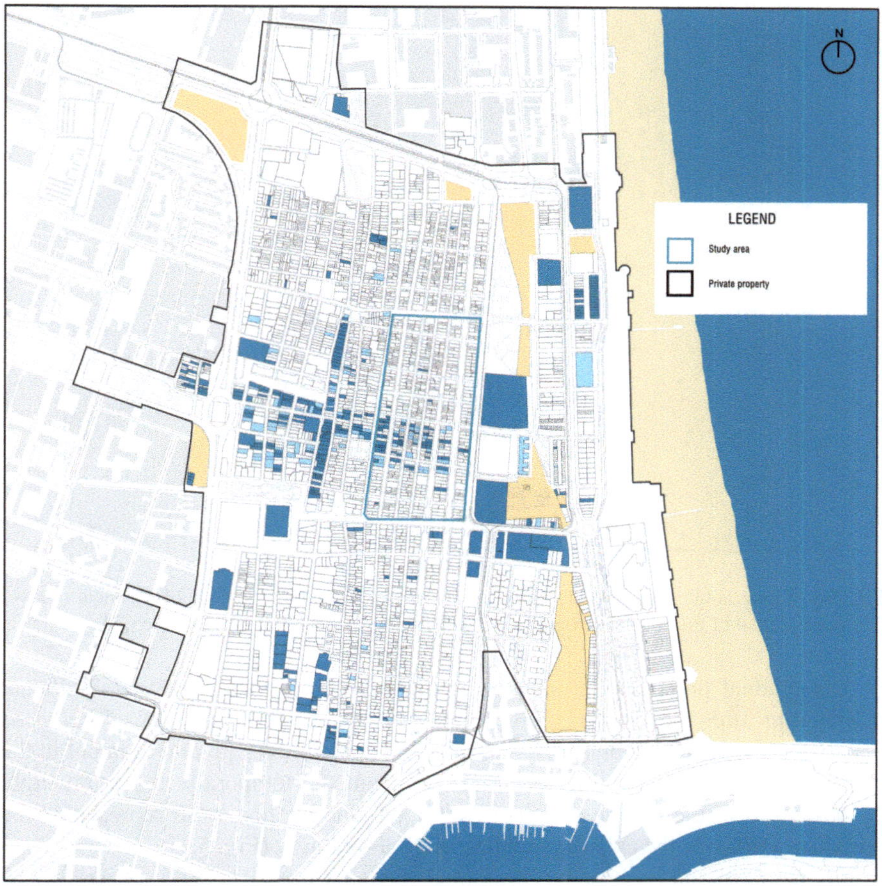

Fig. 5.7 The technical document of the Cabanyal-Canyamelar Special Plan highlights the ownership of buildings and the study area (image created starting from details available on the Valencia City Council website. Link Document (pg. 21) [1])

railway tracks to the north (Castellón). However, currently, the continuity of the urban plot is hindered and interrupted in some areas. The plan (Fig. 5.8) provides a detailed insight into the dwellings' urban structure and the early stages of the architectural transformation that defined the neighbourhood's unique character throughout its history. Out of a total of 568 dwellings, only 56 were built houses, the remainder were huts. In other words, most of the population lived in *barracas* [4]. This building typology provided habitability under the enfiteutic right that governed occupation of these lands. The *barracas* were generally oriented east–west to take full advantage of the sea breeze, a distinctive feature reflected in the 1796 *Topographic Plan of the Población de la Playa de la Ciudad de Valencia*, and a decisive factor in its subsequent expansions.

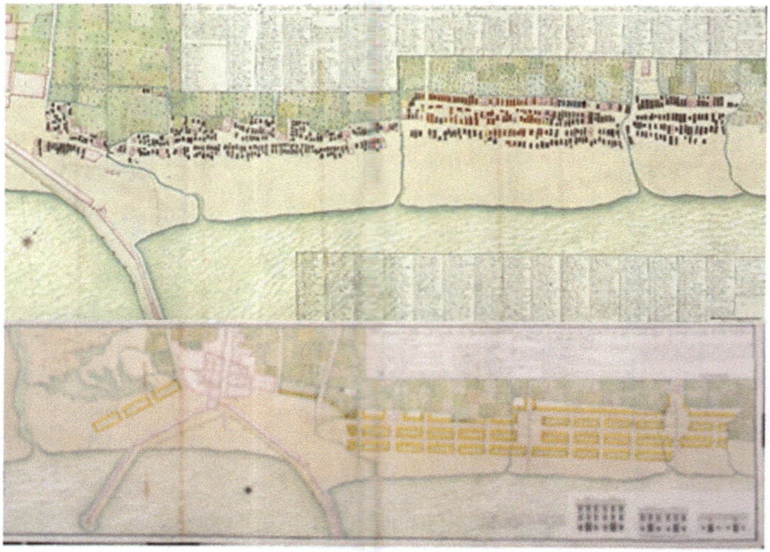

Fig. 5.8 Topographic map of the settlement at the beach area of the City of Valencia (above) Geographic map of the coastal settlement of the City of Valencia (below). (Source: [3])

The gradual process of transforming *barracas* into houses gained significant momentum after the fire of 1796, during which the reconstruction of *barracas* thatched roofs was prohibited. This prohibition constituted a pivotal moment in the district's history, accelerating the transition from the temporary and lightweight constructions of the *barracas* to more solid and durable houses. It represented the initial step towards the existing architectural morphology (Fig. 5.9).

Valencia's inland location has prompted concerns as early as 1865 regarding the connection between the city centre to the sea. Accordingly, in 1865, the first project was drafted to link the city with the maritime settlements [8]. Several projects have been proposed with this aim, without consideration for preserving the neighbourhood's distinctive character. Although none were carried out, they plunged the affected area into a prolonged legal battle, resulting in expropriations, plundering, and demolitions.

Most notably, the Urban Regeneration Plans for the Historic Area (*Plan Especial de Protección y Reforma Integral del Cabanyal-Canyamelar—PEPRI 2001*) posed a serious threat to its historical fabric. Since then, preserving the neighbourhood and its traditions has become a contentious issue, sparking protests and debates over its cultural and architectural identity. In 2009, the Ministry of Culture suspended the *2001 PEPRI*, and in 2016 commissioned the drafting of the *PEC* with a conservation-oriented, urban-regeneration approach, which was subsequently approved in 2023. This process was enriched by previous studies conducted by researchers [7, 9].

Particular emphasis was placed on the analysis of the identified primaeval area, thereby contributing to a deeper understanding of the district's historical and

Fig. 5.9 Historical photo of the neighbourhood of Valencia showing the historical land use and building type of the Barracas. (Source: [5, 6] (above) [7] (below))

technical characteristics. Consequently, an in-depth analysis of descriptors summarised in Tables 4.1, 4.2, 4.3, 4.4, 4.5, and 4.6, such as architectural-constructive-material characteristics, morpho-typological features of the historic built environment, and the morphology of the urban space in the historic district, was undertaken.

The urban environment of the El Cabanyal-Canyamelar district is structured around a system of freely accessible public spaces, originally designed with a primitive street layout adapted to the natural topography of the area.

The distinct maritime character of the district is evident in the arrangement of the streets, which run parallel to the sea in a north-south direction. The urban layout facilitates optimal access to the dwellings, designed to ensure façades receive sunlight at specific times during the day, while the urban pavements benefit from periods of shade.

These streets harmoniously integrate with the routes, promoting permeability between the city and the neighbourhood, and between the latter and the sea. The street layout has been strategically planned, incorporating crossings that create open spaces in the part nearest to the sea. This design facilitates convenient access to the beach, a crucial location for the local fishing industry and, during the summer, also for tourist use. To the west of the district, paths and streets lead towards the city centre.

The symbiosis between the urban fabric and the natural environment, particularly the sea, is a distinctive element of the district. Indeed, the daily lives of El Cabanyal-Canyamelar residents were closely intertwined with the sea, with the streets reflecting their connection to maritime activities, ranging from the fishing industry (*Casa dels Bous, Lonja del Pescado*, among others) to the enjoyment of the beach during the summer months.

The built environment of the El Cabanyal-Canyamelar district derives from its architectural-urban transformation. As shown in Fig. 5.10, the neighbourhood was initially characterised by the typical skyline of *barracas*, with alignments of triangular fronts separated by service spaces intended for the maintenance of the north–south-oriented double-pitched roofs of the *barracas,* known as *escalà.*

However, after the most devastating fire of 1875, which led to the destruction of approximately 250 *barracas*, the municipal administration prohibited the construction of new *barracas* with thatched roofs precisely due to their typological, constructive, and material characteristics, which conferred a high vulnerability to the risk of fire [12]. This resulted in the replacement of wood and earth with brick, and

Fig. 5.10 Historical photo showing the building type of the Barracas and the particular building component of the Escalas. (Source: (above) [10]; below [11])

thatch roofing with clay materials. On a morpho-typological level, the process of replacing *barracas* with brick buildings represented a significant change in the urban layout of the historic neighbourhood. The original façade width had to be preserved if there was still an adjacent *barracas* with a pitched roof, or a slightly greater façade width was permitted if the neighbouring buildings had already been replaced, allowing the new construction to occupy the width of the former *barracas* plus the *escalà*—provided there was agreement among neighbours. Otherwise, the gap between buildings remained empty. This regulatory framework led to a prolonged period of coexistence between *barracas* and their replacements (Fig. 5.10).

In detail, a *barracas* was built on an area of approximately 6.40 m × 10.50 m, within which the only dimensions that could change were the width of the *barraca* front and/or the *escalà*. Currently, the most common building front widths are 6.40/7.08 m and 7.08/7.76 m taking into account the construction status of the adjoining plots. Thus, starting from the building type of the *barracas*, the typological process of buildings presents a series of evolutionary phases (Table 5.1). Initially, the basic type was the single-storey terraced house. It underwent duplication at both planimetric and elevation levels. As the process progressed, the single-family terraced house evolved into a multi-family terraced house, through the duplication of the base cell and the use of cell overlap in height. This evolution led to the creation of a house with two dwellings per floor. This diversity has resulted in a range of architectural styles and details, reflecting both individual preferences and the cultural influences of the respective construction periods (Fig. 5.11).

The coexistence of styles, materials, and architectural details contributes to bestowing upon El Cabanyal-Canyamelar a unique identity and historical appearance. Amidst the architectural complexity of El Cabanyal-Canyamelar, a consistent feature inherited from the village persists: the direct connection of buildings to the street, without common intermediate elements. This direct link reflects a tradition of proximity and social interaction originating from the *barracas* era, when community life predominantly unfolded outdoors. This dynamic has persevered and evolved over time, influencing how the neighbourhood's inhabitants interact with their built environment. Lastly, the dwellings maintain the tradition of a direct relationship with the street, without the interposition of common elements such as entrances or condominium staircases. In the evolution process of the district, the persistence of the terraced house building type (BT) is clearly observed.

In Pastor Villa RM (2016) [13], the morpho-typological analysis of the historical building is comprehensively presented and discussed, providing functional data to use for the work aims.

In detail, sub-types can be inferred in relation to the number of floors and housing units, including:

BT1—Single-Family Terraced House (Fig. 5.12), characterised by a façade width ranging from 3.20 to 7.76 m, a building height of one or two storeys, and an internal distribution of rooms that varies depending on the position of the corridor. The single-family terraced building typology has three subcategories:

Table 5.1 Morpho-typological evolution of the buildings and plots based on the basic unit: the barraca and its escalàs. (Source: [4])

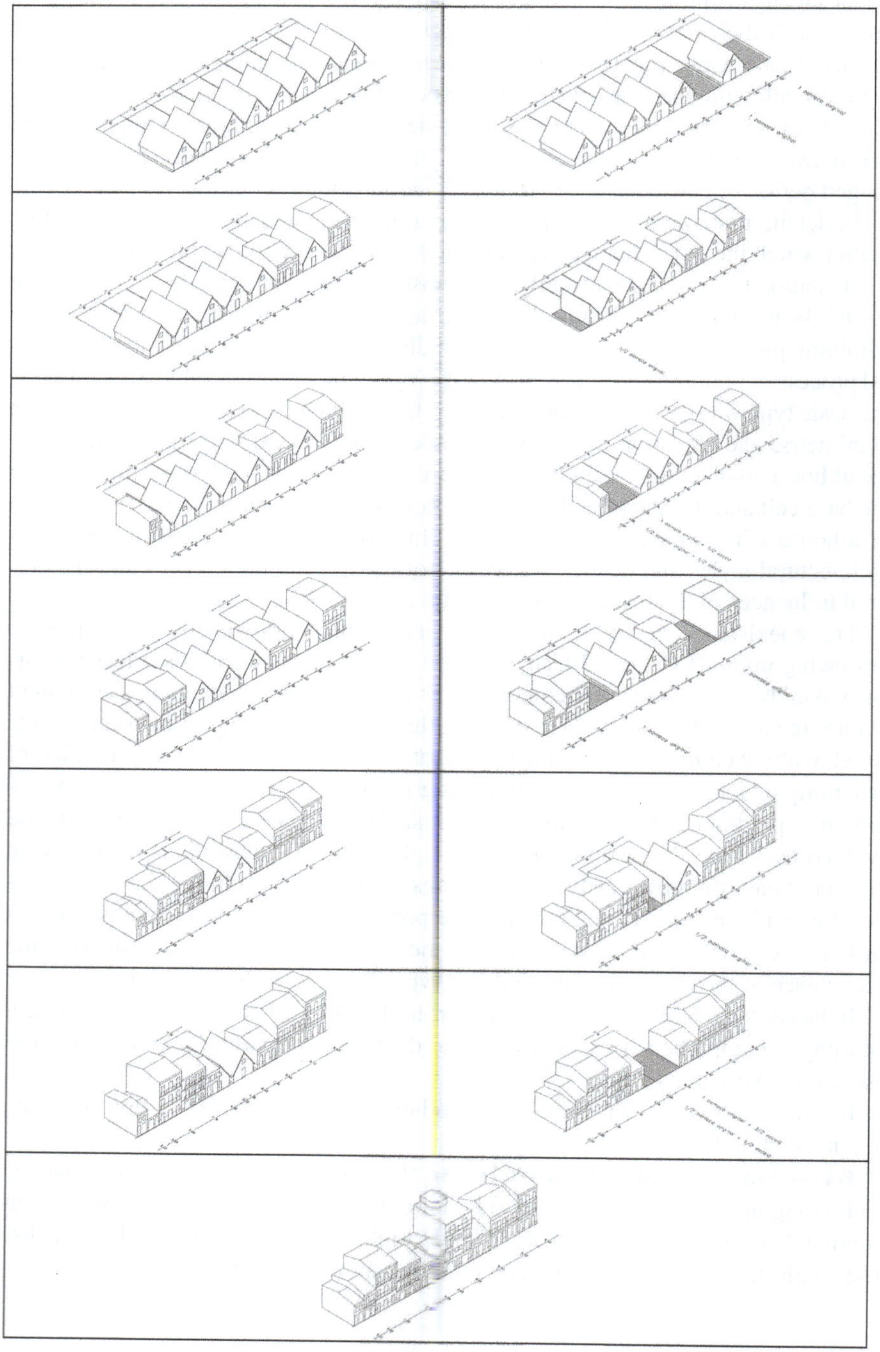

Fig. 5.11 Significant parts of the historical buildings in the historic area of El Cabanyal-Canyamelar neighbourhood

- BT1.1—one-storey Terraced House. The layout is characterised by a lateral and/or central distributor space. The main access space to the dwelling consists of a single room illuminated by the presence of two openings on the main façade: the entrance door and a narrow longitudinal window. The corridor extends from the side or centre of this room, providing access to the bedrooms, which are generally two in number, to the last room, the dining room. From the dining room/kitchen there is access to the inner courtyard of the building. The bathroom, consisting only of the latrine, is located in the inner courtyard.
- BT1.2—one-storey Terraced House with attic. This building type shares the same planimetric characteristics as BT1.1, with the addition of a room on the upper floor, corresponding to the attic or terrace. Access to the attic is provided by a stairwell, the position of which may change in plan.

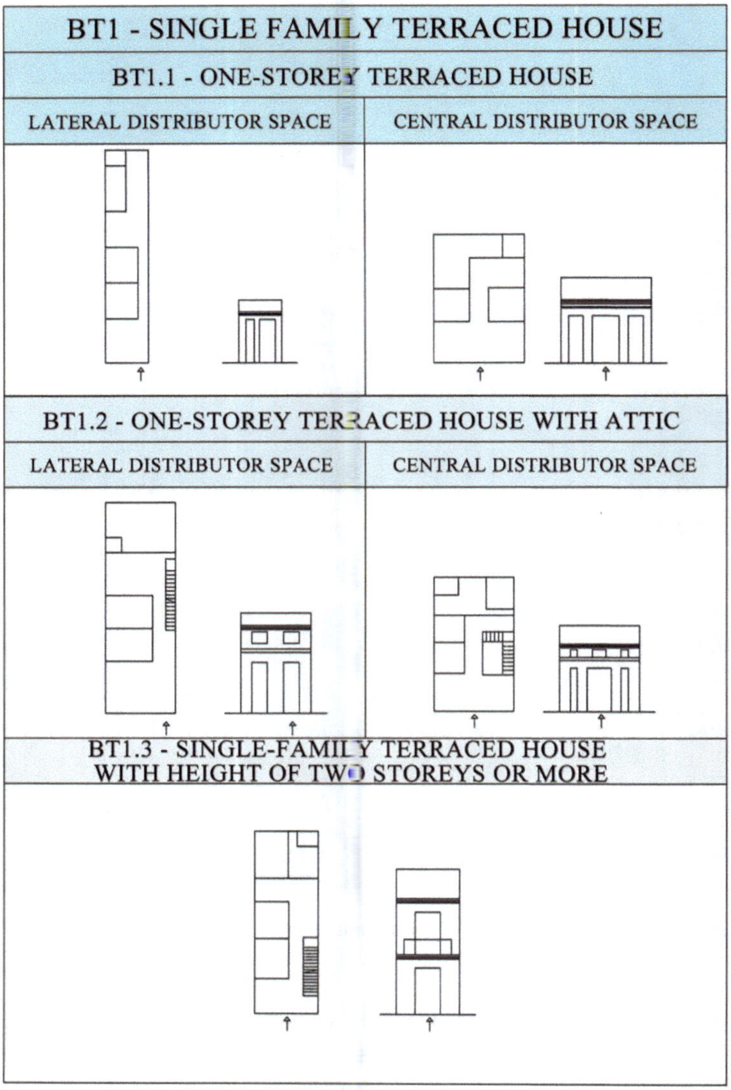

Fig. 5.12 Details of plan distribution of terraced house, for single cell (image created starting from details available on the Valencia City Council website and in [4, 13])

- BT1.3—single-family Terraced House with a height of two storeys or more. This building type retains the planimetric characteristics of BT1.1, with a second floor added. In detail, the presence of a second floor incorporates the architectural element of the balcony and its railing.

BT2—Terraced Multi-family House (Fig. 5.13), a building type consisting of a stairwell that provides access to one dwelling unit per floor.

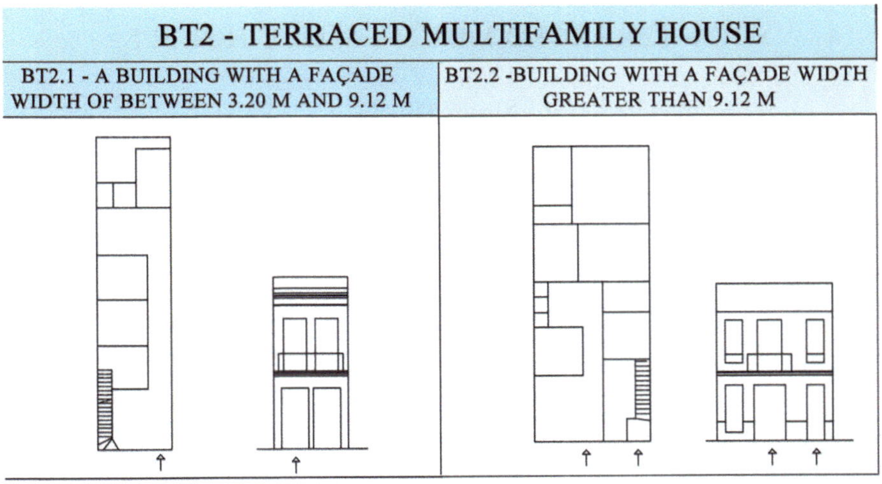

Fig. 5.13 Details of plan distribution of terraced multi-family house (image created starting from details available on the Valencia City Council website and in [4, 13])

The planimetric distribution of the interior rooms follows the same scheme as BT1. The BT2 building type has two subcategories, depending on the width of the main façade and the number of storeys:

- BT2.1—building with a façade width of between 3.20 and 9.12 m and a height of two or three storeys. Type BT 2.1 can have a planimetric layout consisting of a lateral linear staircase and a lateral or central distributor shaft.
- BT2.2—building with a façade width greater than 9.12 m and a number of storeys greater than 2 and a stairwell of two or more flights, on which the internal distribution of rooms depends.

BT3—Terraced Multi-family Houses (Fig. 5.14), a building type characterised by a stairwell that provides access to at least two residential units per floor. The layout distribution varies according to the type (one or more flights) and the position of the stairwell (central or side). Accordingly, three subcategories can be distinguished:

- BT3.1—terraced multi-family house with linear, central staircase and side corridor. The internal room distribution follows the planimetric scheme of BT1.1.
- BT3.2—terraced multi-family house with linear and central staircase and distribution space.
- BT 3.3—terraced multi-family house with two-flight staircase and lateral corridor.

The current configuration of the buildings, respecting the inherited subdivision, has adapted their heights to changing regulations and the needs of the owners. This adaptation has led to a variety of heights between the buildings.

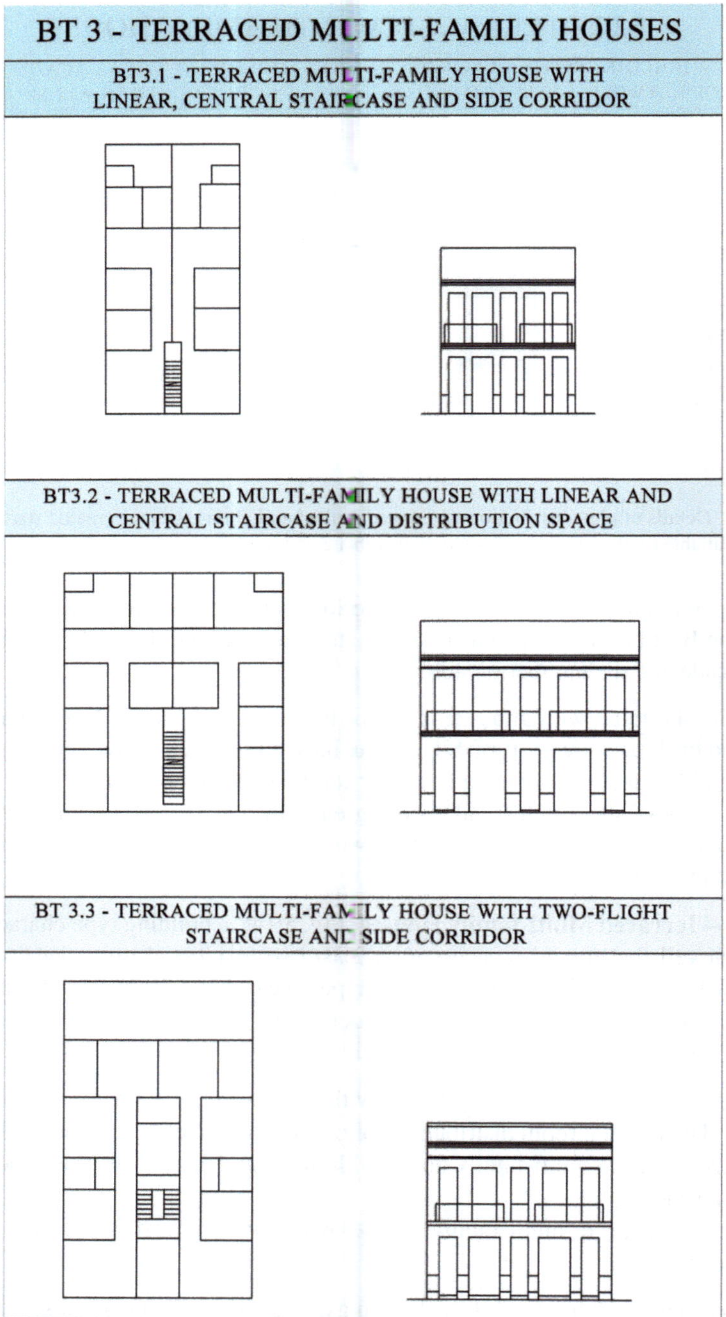

Fig. 5.14 Details of plan distribution of terraced multi-family house consisting of a stairwell serving at least two residential units per floor (image created starting from details available on the Valencia City Council website and in [4, 13])

Additionally, the buildings have inner courtyards that provide double exposure of the interior spaces, and represent a substantial change in the concept of privacy and organisation of space. This feature, resulting from the presence of street frontages and rear courtyards, facilitates effective ventilation of the rooms.

Taking advantage of the regime of sea breezes from east to west, this arrangement favours air exchange and contributes to living comfort. The façades of the houses are finished according to the owners' taste.

Within this context, Phases 1-2-3 of the digital code of practice outlined in Chap. 4 have been applied and validated on the study area of the historic neighbourhood El Cabanyal-Canyamelar in Valencia (Spain). Specifically, particular attention was paid to the spherical-image survey phase (ph 1.3) and on-desk data acquisition using the WebGiSystem and WebVrModel (Ph 3). Consequently, with respect to the first phase of the digital code of practice, an in-depth knowledge of the property under study was conducted (ph 1.1) through the consultation of historical documentation (manuscripts, miscellanies, books), iconographic representations, graphic works (maps, cartographies, and drawings) and historical photographs, from different periods. Additionally, territorial-scale information (orthophoto, regional technical maps, general and detailed urban planning instruments) is analysed and acquired, providing essential input for subsequent geolocation and GiSystem processing.

Based on the outcomes of the historical/archival research, and specifically on the analysis of the large-scale design drawings, the spherical photo acquisition procedure was defined, as well as the relevant survey plan with *n* survey points. In detail, the spherical photos were acquired consecutively with a constant step in the plan, following the established acquisition scheme. Once the survey plan was defined, the acquisition of the equirectangular photos was performed in situ using a spherical head (Theta 360) and a tripod (ph 1.3). Subsequently to the characterisation of the built and urban environment, the acquired data were implemented in the GiSystem prepared according to the defined logical-relational schema (ph 1.2). In parallel, the relational information system PostgreSQL (r-DB) with PostGIS extension was structured via the pigAdmin graphic interface. The latter was connected to the GiSystem environment in order to implement in it the technical knowledge acquired in ph 1.1. Here, each building was geolocalised according to the WGS84 global reference system, and the spatial information level was enriched through the integration of alphanumeric data. This step was crucial for enabling the subsequent translation of the dataset into the CityGML standard. Therefore, the data and information from the historical architectural analysis were systematised in the GIS environment, in compliance with the sections and descriptors defined in Tables 4.1, 4.2, 4.3, 4.4, 4.5, and 4.6.

After acquiring all the information and data concerning the historical building and urban element, the VrModel of the study area was created (ph.2.3). In particular, the VrModel was obtained by linking the 568 spherical images acquired according to the survey plan (ph 1.3) (Fig. 5.15). Given the number of scenes and the complexity of the area (in relation to the morphological similarity of the blocks) an interactive orientation map was implemented to support the use of the VrModel.

Fig. 5.15 Representative equirectangular images

This map, enhanced with dedicated hotspots, enables users to select the specific environment to be viewed (Fig. 5.16).

In addition, a specific hotspot was placed within each spherical that allows connection to the WebGiSystem. Similarly, a hotspot was inserted to each building, allowing connection to the specific section of the r-DB (Fig. 5.17).

The generated VrModel was then prepared to be used via the web in a semi-immersive (on-desk) way. Before enabling web sharing, the hyperlink of the WebVrModel was implemented in the r-DB sections. Subsequently, the web sharing of the GiSystem was configured using the QGIS geo-server and the Apache web-server, thus allowing access to technical knowledge information via web browser (Fig. 5.17).

By means of the WebGiSystem and WebVrModel, additional technical knowledge data was implemented into the r-DB, including detailed information on the

Fig. 5.16 VrModel home screen

state of conservation of each building. This proved essential for carrying out the reconnaissance analysis of the study area.

Consistently with the T-DSS rules, buildings characterised by a low level of conservation were identified for further quantitative conservation analysis (Ph. 4). In accordance with phase 4 of the digital code of practice, the photogrammetric survey was carried out. Specifically, the digital survey was conducted through the use of passive terrestrial digital technologies, i.e. camera (Canon EOS 100D) mounted on the tripod/telescopic, useful for the acquisition of portions positioned at high heights. Given the recurring morpho-typological and architectural characteristics of the surveyed buildings, the acquisition procedure was standardised and applied according to a consistent scheme across all identified cases.

Consequently, the frames were processed using Structure from Motion (SfM) software (Agisoft Metashape©), obtaining three-dimensional elements in the form of textured point clouds (Fig. 5.18).

At the end of the elaboration of the three-dimensional models, scale orthophotos of the building façades were generated (Fig. 5.19). These orthophotos provided reliable perspective backdrops, serving as the basis for subsequent GIS-based mapping of degradation through the identification of specific degradation patterns.

The use of Virtual Reality techniques for the acquisition of descriptors proved particularly effective in collecting large amounts of data within a geographic database (GIS, .shp). This database constitutes the core information system to be subsequently translated into the CityGML environment.

Fig. 5.17 Home screen of the WebGiSystem showing the query of an architectural entity. The information window allows the connection to the WebVrModel, as well as the implementation of further data, remotely on-desk, in the r-DB

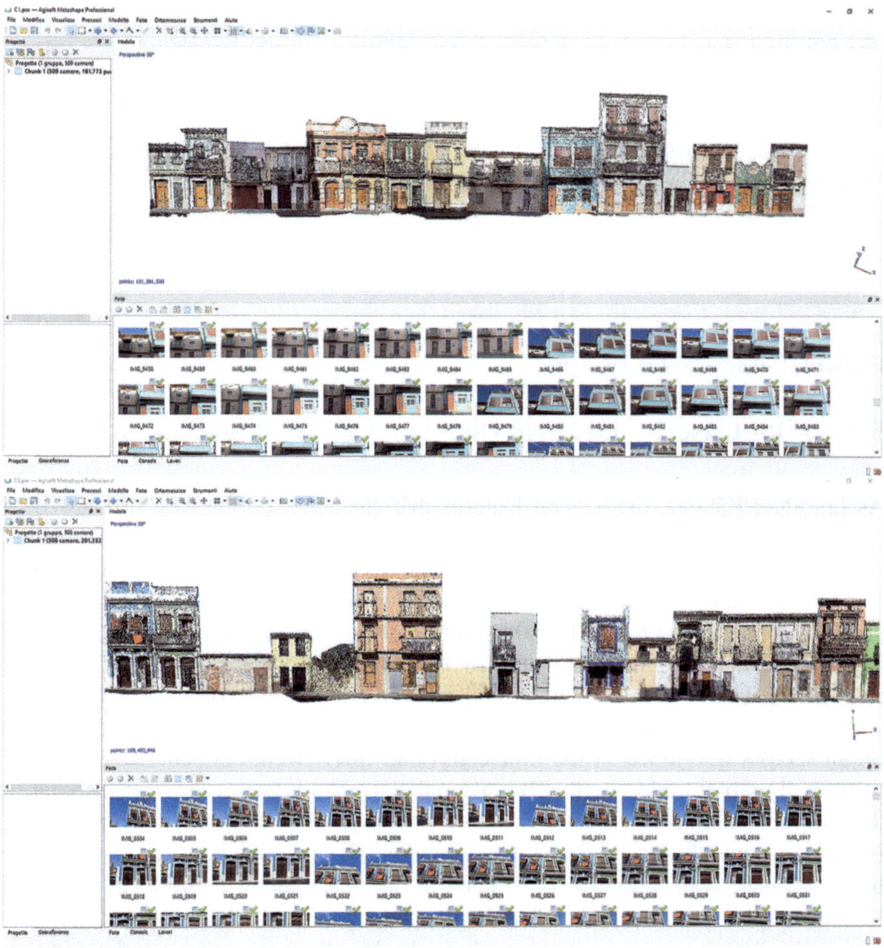

Fig. 5.18 Processing of point clouds of urban fronts using SFM software

Fig. 5.19 Orthophoto of an urban front

5.2 Pilot Case 2—Historic District of Carovigno (Italy)

As introduced above, the general features that characterised the case of Carovigno influenced its selection for the application of the 3hD-DigitalCode, where establishing a CityGML-based 3D urban model provides an opportunity to bridge the present gaps.

The historic district of Carovigno, a town located in the Apulia region of southern Italy, originated on a hill of the south-eastern Murgia plateau, approximately 8 km from the Adriatic coast and 28 km from the provincial capital, Brindisi (Fig. 5.20). The ancient settlement comprises a historic core of Messapian origin, which was later expanded and consolidated during the medieval period, as well as urban sectors developed in the nineteenth and early twentieth centuries featuring historically structured layouts. The original acropolis is believed to correspond to the current ancient core which was accessed through three gateways: *Porta Brindisi*, *Porta Nova*, and *Porta del Prete*. This elliptical-shaped ancient core was enclosed by a defensive wall, initially constructed in the fifth century using local materials such as carparo and limestone. The fortification system was later reinforced—first during the Roman era and subsequently in the Middle Ages—through the addition of four defensive towers, two of which were rectangular and two circular in plan.

The technical survey process of the historic district of Carovigno began with investigations conducted at the municipal authority. A thorough analysis of key descriptors—namely, the architectural, constructional, and material characteristics, the morphological and typological features of the historic built environment, and the urban morphology of the ancient town—revealed the recurrence of similar traits across two distinct urban areas, each corresponding to a different historical phase of foundation. Specifically, the main cognitive elements characterising the homogeneous buildings of the ancient core emerge both at the urban and architectural levels: at the urban scale, the layout is defined by curvilinear pathways, shaped by defensive needs and the distinctive topography of the Carovigno territory; at the architectural scale, the predominant building type is the Terraced House. The urban layout of Carovigno's historic district is primarily composed of an irregular street network, within which it is possible to identify two main traffic axes (oriented North-South and East-West), from which secondary pathways branch off.

Fig. 5.20 Location of Carovigno (BR) in Italy (above) and perimetration of the historic centre in the city land (under), with background map data © OpenStreetMap contributors

Additionally, urban open spaces are located in correspondence with architectural landmarks such as churches and the castle. These open spaces, often paved with stone slabs, serve as public squares situated in front of the castle, the town hall, and other historically significant buildings. In contrast, the remaining open spaces are paved with cement tiles.

The morpho-typological, constructional, and material analysis of the built environment within the historic district led to the identification of four principal building types (BT1–BT4) (Fig. 5.21):

BT1—Terraced House type is the most prevalent across the historic building and is characterised by both single-cell (a) and double-cell (b) configurations, exhibiting either vertical or horizontal development patterns. These variations reflect an evolutionary process, where originally independent housing units were merged to accommodate expanded functional needs. The single-cell configuration (a) typically features a single street-facing façade and consists of one to three interconnected rooms arranged along an axis perpendicular to the road. Vertical dwelling development, when present, is achieved through either an internal staircase—leading to a secondary level and possibly the roof via a service room with flat or pitched roofing—or an external staircase, often accessed via a small elevated vestibule positioned a few steps above street level. These units were historically designed with

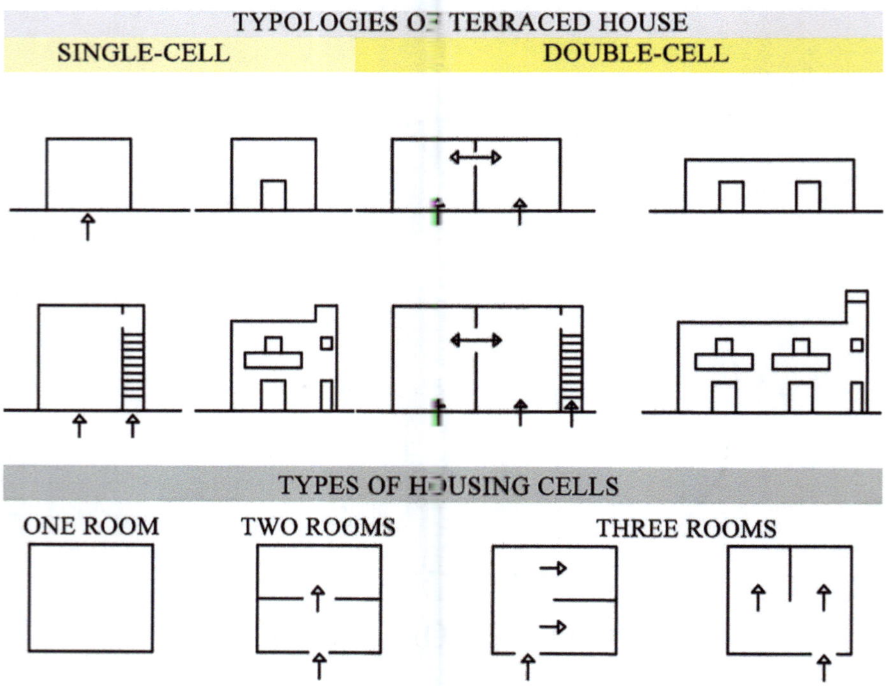

Fig. 5.21 Details of plan distribution of terraced house, for single and double cells (image created starting from details available on the Municipality of Carovigno website. Link [14])

thick load-bearing masonry walls and high ceilings covered by vaulted systems (e.g. barrel or cloister vaults), ensuring structural integrity and thermal mass.

The double-cell configuration (b) involves the horizontal aggregation of two equally sized housing units placed parallel to the street façade. This spatial arrangement improves both natural lighting and air circulation, ensuring that both living and sleeping areas are directly oriented towards the street, thereby addressing the hygienic deficiencies of the single-cell model. In its vertically developed variant, the double-cell house includes internal stairs and typically spans two floors.

BT2—In-Line House represents a multi-family residential typology distinguished by an articulated plan layout and significant volumetric development. These buildings often possess multiple façades and overlook points (balconies or loggias) and were historically developed to accommodate several residential units within a single structure. Vertically organised over two floors, the ground floor was traditionally allocated to non-residential uses such as stables, agricultural storage, or oil presses, while the upper floor served residential purposes. Vertical dwelling development is facilitated by a staircase with a potentially complex configuration, sometimes integrating additional flights to connect rooms with varied floor levels. This typology is often interpreted as a direct architectural evolution of the Terraced House (BT1), offering more diversified spatial articulation and functional hierarchy.

BT3—Palace type shares similar planimetric and volumetric features with the In-Line House (BT2) but is further distinguished by the presence of refined architectural and decorative elements, such as framed windows, ornamental cornices, and wrought-iron balconies. These elements allow the typology to be chronologically attributed to the early twentieth century, aligning with broader architectural transformations of the period. Consequently, the BT3 represents a high-status variant of BT2, reflecting social prestige and stylistic aspirations within the historic urban fabric.

BT4—Corner or End House constitutes a typological variation designed to resolve spatial constraints at urban intersections or block terminations. These structures lack recurring features found in other types but are noteworthy for their adaptive configurations, often incorporating irregular layouts and façades to mediate between adjoining streets or buildings. Their form results from site-specific design responses rather than standardised schemes.

Across all typologies, the construction system is dominated by load-bearing masonry walls, primarily built using local *Leccese* tuff (a soft workable limestone typical of the region). Walls are composed either of a single solid layer or composite masonry, typically left unplastered or plastered, contributing to the textural identity of the built environment.

The roofing systems are generally vaulted, employing structural solutions such as barrel, cloister, and star-shaped vaults, which allowed the creation of robust upper floors while enhancing the spatial performance of interior spaces. The reliance on locally sourced materials and region-specific construction techniques constitutes a core component of the historical and technological identity of Carovigno's historic core (Fig. 5.22).

Fig. 5.22 Significant parts of the historical buildings in the Historic Centre of Carovigno

The 3hD-DigitalCode developed for the case study required a meticulous collection and analysis of theoretical notions, practical experiences, and previous scientific and regulatory studies of the historical area of Carovigno, which were conducted (ph 1.1). The technical knowledge acquired in this phase facilitated the encoding of the collected data according to the ontological structure (ph 1.2), as well as their archival storage in r-DB (ph 2.2) connected to the GiSystem (ph. 2.1).

In the detail of data and activities in ph 1.1, geometric and spatial information of buildings are extracted from the Regional Technical Charter (SIT Apulia Region), while morpho-typological, constructive, and architectural features have been collected starting from in situ surveys and previous studies and technical activities. These data are thus used to set up the basic geographic information system of the historic district (Fig. 5.23). Here, the architectural entities have been represented with vector polygons in the global reference system (WGS84-UTM 33N) and the r-DB has been structured through attribute tables (ph 1.2) (Figs. 5.23 and 5.24).

In particular, a specific attribute table has been created for each section of the r-DB, structured to support: (1) the historic-archival information (Ph 1); (2) the data acquired on-desk (Ph 3); and (3) the conservation level by thematic mapping (Ph 4). Simultaneously, the spherical image survey (ph 1.3) was conducted in accordance with the prescribed acquisition plan, where 725 points were captured at a consistent interval in the planimetry.

Specifically, the equirectangular photos were acquired on-site using a spherical head (Samsung GEAR 360 camera) and a tripod. Following this, the VrModel was generated by interconnecting the captured images in ph. 1.3. Moreover, a dynamic orientation map has been incorporated in each scene, enabling the user to navigate through the scene and ascertain its planimetric localisation.

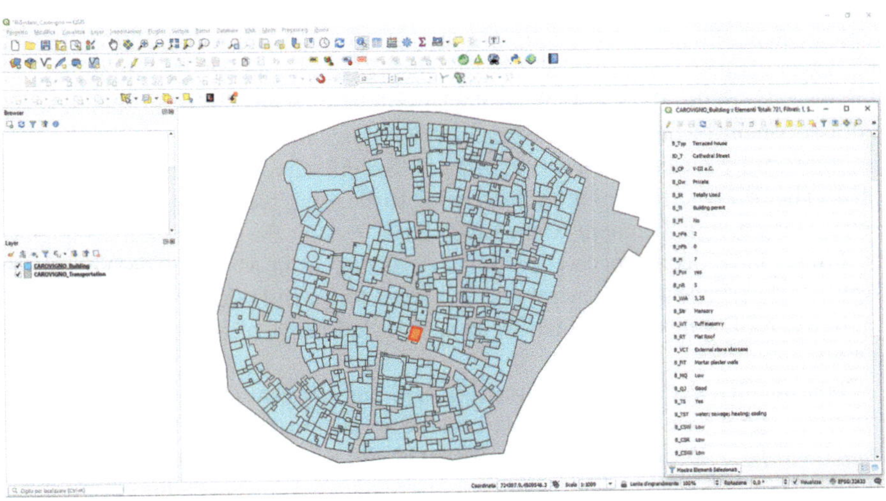

Fig. 5.23 GiSystem of the Historic Centre of Carovigno. On the right, the information window showing the descriptors implemented in the r-DB for the selected building

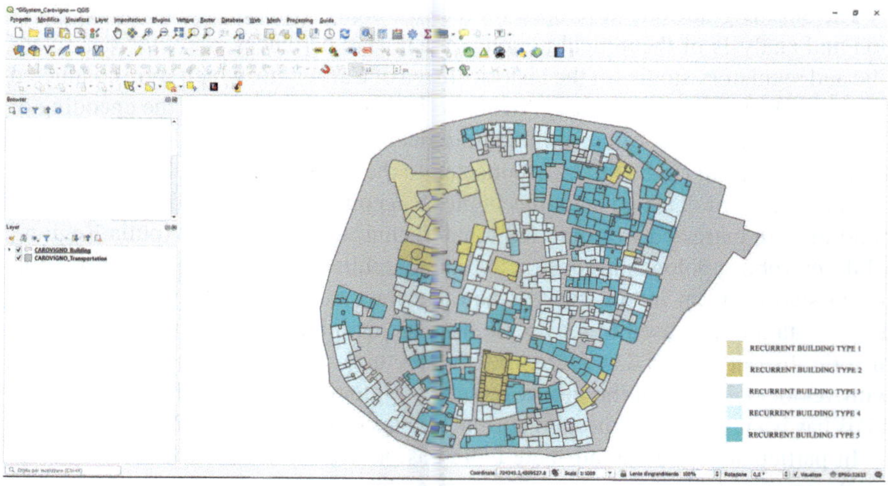

Fig. 5.24 GiSystem of the Historic Centre of Carovigno showing recurring architectural types

The orientation map also facilitates the viewing of the *n* acquisition points on the site, enabling users to navigate within the virtual model. Additionally, each scene includes a hotspot connecting to the WebGiSystem for its use. Specifically for the VrModel, individual hotspots have been incorporated for each building and urban element, allowing a connection to the r-DB. Consequently, both the GiSystem and the VrModel have been adapted for web-based access (Ph3).

Thus, all the technical knowledge and information pertaining to the reconnaissance analysis of the conservative state of the historic building were acquired in a semi-immersive, web-based manner at the desk. During this process, the r-DB was implemented with all the pertinent information necessary for identifying buildings and urban elements requiring a more detailed examination (Ph. 4), in alignment with the rules of the T-DSS. As far as the latter is concerned (Ph4), the qualification and assessment of decays for the selected buildings have been processed in GIS environment by means of their orthoimages. Specifically, the image-based survey (ph 4.1) has been performed in situ according to the principles of digital photogrammetry, using a digital camera (Canon EOS 100D). After the acquisition campaign, the frames have been processed within a Structure from Motion (SfM) software (Agisoft Metashape©) to generate orthoimages for each building sub-component (masonry, roof, windows), which were then scaled using measurements acquired in situ.

Subsequently, decays was identified in GIS environment (ph 4.2), using vector primitives, geolocated and associated to the related architectural entities in the shapefile (Fig. 5.25). Details on each decay (B_Td, B_S, B_In, B_Ex) and for each building sub-component were recorded in the associated attribute table in the r-DB, completing the implementation of data in the GIS environment.

The analysis of the state of conservation of the wall structures revealed a widespread condition of degradation, attributable to both environmental factors and

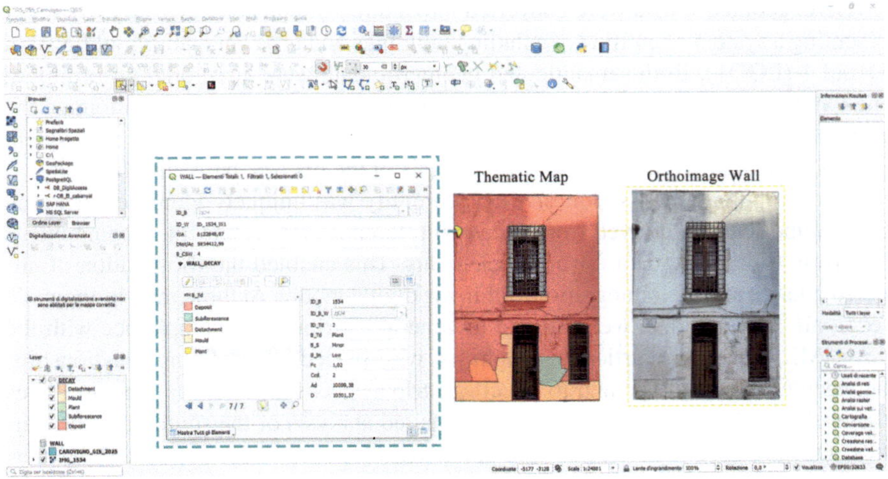

Fig. 5.25 Thematic map of the exposed wall of a building

inadequate maintenance. The principal forms of decay mapped include: (1) generalised surface deposits, composed of atmospheric particulates, dust, and organic matter, which compromise the material integrity and alter the chromatic perception of the wall surfaces; (2) plaster detachment in the basement areas, leading to exposure of the underlying masonry, often accompanied by mould colonies, indicative of prolonged moisture retention; (3) efflorescence in localised areas, suggesting the presence of capillary rising damp and the migration of soluble salts through the masonry fabric; and (4) plants at various points along the elevation, further contributing to the deterioration of the structural and aesthetic condition of the walls. For roofs, the main form of decay identified are biological patina and degradation of the roof covering. For windows, a low state of conservation of the shading elements has been identified, and the degradation of the wooden doors caused by the presence of dampness, and the breakage/absence of glass.

Subsequently, for each sub-component, the graphical-vector representation of the state of conservation has been produced, representing the areas of decay with vector polygons. Therefore, each vector polygon mapped on the ortho-image has been related to the *Conservation level* in the corresponding r-DB section. In this process, the logical relationships are configured, and the calculator fields have been prepared to allow: (1) the identification of the type of decay, from the defined choice set; (2) the definition of the severity and level of degradation; and (3) the calculation of the decay extension, codifying it in alphanumeric attributes. The calculated fields prepared in the specific tables, as well as according to the equations (Sect. 4.2), allowed the automatic compilation of the field relating to the primary factor of the state of conservation of each component of single architectures. Consequently, the CityGML-based model has been created within the Safe FME visual programming platform, according to the specific defined workbenches.

Here, geometric data were converted into a three-dimensional digital model representing a system of entities—including buildings and urban elements—at Level of Detail 1 (LOD1). Both semantic and geometric data were structured according to the CityGML standard, while logical functions were implemented to automate the processing of primary and derived indicators, thereby supporting the subsequent phases of qualitative and quantitative analysis of the historic built environment.

During the parametrisation phase, each entity was uniquely identified using an alphanumeric code, derived from cadastral references for architectural components and from toponymic data for urban elements. This enabled the formulation of targeted queries and their integration within the digital model. At the semantic-thematic level, all collected data were filtered to generate attributes in compliance with the CityGML standard. Particular emphasis was placed on defining relationships between each entity type and its specific attributes, as well as among the attributes themselves. This was achieved through detailed analysis of the source data properties, accounting for both the intrinsic characteristics of the information and the hierarchical relationships—vertical, between classes, and horizontal, among attributes within a given CityGML class. Consequently, architectural entities were assigned to the *Building* class, while urban elements were incorporated into the *Transportation* class. Additional attributes were expressed using the CityGML *Generic Attribute* class, in accordance with the relevant datatype. The final output was a geometric and semantic-thematic model structured according to the CityGML standard, representing the semantic digital model of the historic core of Carovigno.

The CityGML-based model created (ph 5.1) has been imported and archived within 3DCityDB, using PostgreSQL as a relational database with its PostGIS extension. The use of 3DCityDB (ph 5.2) has allowed the export of the geometric model (.json) and the semantic data (.csv) for subsequent visualisation and use in a web environment, as well as the management of archived data over time. In this way, the model is set up to be used in a web environment within the Cesium virtual globe. Within the 3DCityDB Web Map Client platform (Phase 6), individual architectural buildings can be queried either semantically—by executing targeted searches based on unique attribute values—or geometrically, through the direct selection of a specific model (Fig. 5.26). In both cases, the platform enables the display of semantic information related to the selected object via a pop-up window. Furthermore, a thematic 3D map was developed to illustrate the priority levels for building interventions. Regarding data visualisation, the pop-up window shown on the right side of Fig. 5.26 presents all catalogued and structured information for the selected building. Particular emphasis is placed on the *WebVrModel_link* attribute, which includes an HTTP link that enables users to access and interact with the building in a web-based virtual reality environment.

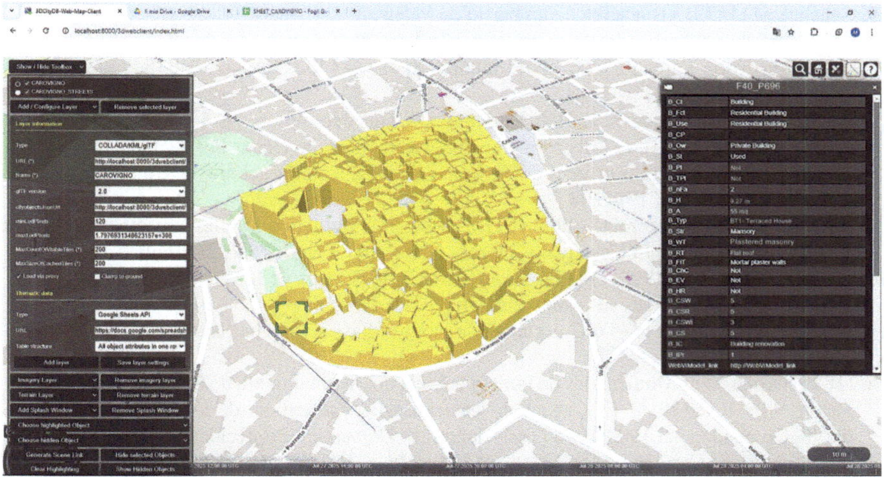

Fig. 5.26 Visualisation of the parametric model in the 3DCityDB Web Map Client and visible details of the selected building in the pop-up window on the right

5.3 Final Remarks on Method Validation

The application of the Digital Code of Practice to the two emblematic pilot cases demonstrates its potential to transform the way architectural built heritage is documented, analysed, and managed. By integrating semantic information systems and CityGML-based and VR-based models, the research has shown how digital tools can streamline procedures, reduce operational gaps, and enhance the technical understanding of complex historic districts. Ultimately, the validation of the Digital Code of Practice emerges as a scalable and adaptable protocol, capable of fostering collaboration among professionals and public institutions while opening new perspectives for the preservation of architectural built heritage in the digital age.

Acknowledgements The authors thank the Valencia City Council and the Municipality of Carovigno for allowing access to technical data.

References

1. (2016) PLANOS DE INFORMACIÓN. PEP Cabanyal-Canyamelar. https://www.valencia.es/ayuntamiento/urbanismo2.nsf/0/530911BD607A303CC125840F0043DA3C/$FILE/223-2016PlanosInformación.PEPCabanyal-Canyamelar_firmado.pdf?OpenElement. Accessed 30 July 2025
2. Terol TS (2014) El Cabanyal: un barrio patrimonial a rehabilitar. Universitat de València
3. Sambricio C (1991) Territorio y ciudad en la España de la Ilustración
4. (2023) Memoria informativa. Plan especial del Cabanyal-Canyamelar y su entorno urbano. Texto refundido

5. Sánchez M (1858) Vista aérea de un barrio de Valencia
6. Vista área de un barrio de Valencia. https://coleccionmun.unav.edu/objects/6859/vista-area-de-un-barrio-de-valencia?ctx=c9df3dde6[illegible]4c3e983444d9ca4d08a7a0ab35d7c9&idx=15. Accessed 30 July 2025
7. Kazimierczak J, Wrona K (2019) Regeneration and demolition vis-á-vis disintegration of urban space: the case of el Cabanyal-Canyamelar in Valencia. Geogr Pol 92:121
8. i Maiques JVB (2000) Els orígens del Passeig de València al Mar: el proyecte de Manuel Sorní de 1865. Cuad Geogr, 191–208
9. Basset-Salom L, Guardiola-Víllora A (2021) Seismic vulnerability and expected damage in "ground zero area" in El Cabanyal (Valencia). Int J Archit Herit 15:1623–1640
10. Gosálvez Gómez V (1998) Estudio constructivo de la Barraca de la Vega Valenciana. Facs. ed. manuscrito original. Facs ed manuscrito Orig
11. Barberà Masip V (1875) Colección de fotografías sobre barracas valencianas. Bibl Valencia Digit
12. (1875) Ordenanzas Municipales de Policía Urbana del Ayuntamiento de Pueblo Nuevo del Mar
13. Pastor Villa RM (2016) El Cabanyal: lectura de las estructuras de la edificación. ensayo tipológico residencial 1900-1936 [Tesis doctoral]. Universitat Politècnica de València
14. Municipality of Carvigno (2023) General Urban Plan (P.U.G.), in compliance with the PPTR and the PAI. https://www.comune.carovigno.br.it/it/documenti_pubblici/piano-urbanistico-generale-p-u-g-adeguamento-al-pptr-ed-al-pai-adozione-2023. Accessed 30 July 2025

Chapter 6
Final Perspectives on Integrated Digital Strategies for Heritage Conservation and Management

Abstract The final result is reported, which allows the dissemination of knowledge during all the phases of the conservation process among the different actors involved, as well as creating a link between institutional-scientific bodies and public bodies in the planning and design phases of interventions for the recovery of architectural heritage, solving critical issues related to the abandonment, physical degradation, and functional obsolescence.

Keywords Preservation strategies · Integrated conservation · Interdisciplinary collaboration · Parametric modelling in conservation · Digital heritage

Historical urban areas represent complex components of our Cultural Heritage, requiring thorough analysis, understanding, and valorisation. Their complexity arises from the interplay of the multiple disciplines involved and the different temporal and spatial scales that characterise these contexts. In this scenario, the management of technical knowledge and data presents a dual challenge: among the actors involved in the process and across the different phases of conservation. Within the regulatory landscape, the lack of standardisation of preservation procedures is evident and can be attributed to several factors. Firstly, the critical nature of the theoretical notions involved makes it difficult to establish universal guidelines. Secondly, the architectural complexity of the existing heritage contributes to the challenge, requiring flexible and adaptable approaches. Finally, the fragmentation of technical knowledge across disciplines adds a further layer of complication, as it is often necessary to integrate approaches from different fields. The need to rethink the conservation process is clear, motivating collaborative efforts between experts from multiple disciplines, the development of flexible methodologies, and the promotion of conceptual frameworks aligned with regulations, which consider the complexity and diversity of historic districts [1].

The management and understanding of existing built heritage present intrinsic challenges characterised by uncertainty, complexity, and multi-scalar dimensions. Effectively addressing these challenges requires approaches that operate across

M. Lasorella et al., *Architectural Heritage Management via Digital Code of Practice*, SpringerBriefs in Architectural Design and Technology,
https://doi.org/10.1007/978-981-95-5106-4_6

multiple levels and engage a variety of disciplinary fields. Such approaches are essential for comprehensive analysis, the identification of context-specific factors, and the selection of appropriate intervention strategies. Uncertainty arises from the broad spectrum of variables influencing the building stock, including structural conditions, regulatory frameworks, environmental constraints, and functional requirements. Complexity stems from the interdependence of these factors and the necessity to account for their dynamic interactions [2].

Nevertheless, the advancement of state-of-the-art surveying techniques—such as laser scanning and digital photogrammetry—alongside the development of parametric digital modelling environments (e.g. BIM/HBIM and 3D City Models), as well as the integration of Virtual Reality technologies, has led to the emergence of new survey scenarios and operational protocols [3–5]. These protocols rely on structured models capable of representing historical artefacts across multiple levels of information. As a result, the role of three-dimensional digital models—whether image—or VR-based—and of Spatial Information Systems (GIS-based) has become increasingly central to the cognitive, diagnostic, and conservation processes [6].

Within this context, the conservation of architectural heritage demonstrates several key strengths that support the preservation and enhancement of existing structures:

- Cultural heritage preservation. Conservation efforts aim to safeguard the cultural assets of a community or society, ensuring the protection of historically valuable artefacts, buildings, and sites for future generations. This process reinforces the identity value of places, fostering a deeper community connection with its heritage and an understanding of societal evolution [7].
- Environmental sustainability. The rehabilitation of existing structures significantly reduces the environmental footprint compared to new construction. It entails lower resource consumption and waste generation, aligning with principles of sustainability [8].
- Adaptability and flexibility. Existing architectural structures often exhibit a capacity for adaptation to new functional demands without compromising their historical character. This inherent flexibility supports evolving societal needs over time [9].

Despite these advantages, the conservation of built heritage also presents notable challenges and limitations, including:

- Complexity of technical knowledge. Effective conservation frequently demands specialised expertise in traditional construction methods and historical architectural analysis [10].
- Absence of standardisation and unstructured decision-making. Traditional cognitive and methodological approaches in conservation are not standardised with respect to objective parameters (such as period of construction, current condition, or architectural typology), affecting both the operational execution of conservation and the interpretation of its outcomes (e.g. restoration plans, urban regeneration programmes). The formulation of intervention strategies lacks stan-

dardised methodologies, as it must account for a wide range of parameters in prioritising actions [11, 12].

- Changing conditions. Conservation efforts are often challenged by dynamic factors such as environmental changes, natural disasters, or human activity, which can compromise the long-term effectiveness of strategies [13, 14].

To overcome these criticalities, multi-level strategies are essential, encompassing detailed analyses across various scales, from the urban fabric to individual architectural elements. Moreover, an interdisciplinary approach involving historical, architectural, structural, and conservation domains is vital to develop a comprehensive understanding of the challenges involved. Such multi-scalar and multidisciplinary methodologies enable the development of innovative, context-sensitive solutions [15]. Within this framework, the management of built heritage must adopt a holistic perspective one that transcends routine maintenance, incorporating cultural and social dimensions, both past and present. Conservation planning must therefore reconcile the principles of *maintenance* with those of *conservation*, embedding them within broader heritage management strategies [16].

The analysis of an architectural artefact should be framed within a broader perspective, where the performance of technological components is evaluated not against the standardised benchmarks applied to new constructions, but rather against acceptable performance thresholds to define appropriate maintenance and conservation measures [17]. The effective understanding and management of the existing built heritage demand an integrated approach that combines diverse competencies and methodologies, enabling the development of intervention strategies that are sustainable, resilient, and adaptable. It is crucial to highlight that the success of conservation efforts depends on thorough planning, the active engagement of local communities, and the adoption of flexible strategies that respect both the cultural value and the practical requirements of conservation [18]. Accordingly, identifying and correlating key factors contributing to the fragility and vulnerability of an artefact—including cultural and historical values—is essential [19]. This analytical perspective aligns with the broader framework of assessing conservation condition levels, thereby supporting informed and context-sensitive decision-making.

Recent scientific studies have deepened and demonstrated the importance of standardised parametric models in architectural and building activities, emphasising their fundamental usefulness in the systematisation of technical knowledge for both simple and complex cases. Such models ensure accurate representation at both geometric and semantic levels, facilitated by interoperability among survey and modelling tools and techniques, and the structuring of semantic and geometric models based on widespread and thematic ontologies [20].

The effectiveness of these models is further enhanced when historical and cultural significance contribute to the basic understanding of Cultural Heritage, regardless of its uniqueness or presence in the urban landscape. The urban-architectural layout of historic districts represents a category of Cultural Heritage, where significance derives from the ensemble of architectural elements rather than a single asset. These elements are crucial for preserving historical continuity, despite the limited interest shown by major administrative bodies in addressing the issue. Recovery plans often stem from assessing urban residential needs, with data collection and processing being time-consuming and labour-intensive, requiring experts to analyse historical, archival, and technological evidence for multiple urban areas. The objective is to identify levels of intervention and related priorities in a systematic set of rules and possible solutions in an integrated way. Within this complex framework, the state of conservation of a historic district plays a key role in the management and selection of conservation actions [21].

This study provides a comprehensive overview of the complexity involved in developing a structured and integrated digital code to support the conservation process, specifically through the application of the CityGML standard. The research underpinning this contribution also addresses the standardisation of conservation procedures, with a particular focus on the phases of data acquisition and the systematisation of technical knowledge required for defining intervention strategies at the scale of urban districts. The proposed digital code of practice is based on a three-dimensional CityGML-based model, which is integrated with a technical decision support system (T-DSS). The resulting conceptual framework, referred to as the 3D Historic District Digital Code (3hD-DigitalCode), supports the formulation of conservation strategies for historic urban areas. This approach harnesses the capabilities of CityGML, a standardised format for representing 3D urban and landscape models, by embedding it within a systematic conservation-oriented methodology tailored to historic districts.

The research outlines a structured operational and methodological workflow that leverages innovative tools and approaches for the organisation and management of complex, multi-layered knowledge systems. Data and information are systematised through defined logical-relational schemas, enabling the automatic generation of additional attributes via analytical processes conducted across multiple scales of analysis, ranging from individual elements and components to entire buildings and urban structures. This approach supports the creation of a standardised and integrated digital model in which data are fully interoperable, accessible, and usable by both professionals in the field and public authorities. In detail, the digital code of practice is therefore conceived as a strategic support tool for local administrations, facilitating the prioritisation of conservation interventions and the planning of subsequent enhancement processes.

The code is built upon the CityGML framework for the representation and management of neighbourhood-scale urban environments and is enhanced by a comprehensive reporting system for evaluating the conservation status of the built heritage.

The approach exploits CityGML's integrability with an external information system (T-DSS), governed by logical-mathematical rules aligned with recognised standards (UNI EN 16096:2012; UNI CEN TS 17385:2019) and intervention classification. The resulting digital code of practice, structured through a procedural flow composed of sequential steps and sub-steps, provides a robust foundation for digital recovery plan development. The operational and methodological framework is designed to accommodate both innovative and traditional techniques for assessing the conservation condition. Additionally, the implementation of T-DSS rules within the FME transformation environment enables the creation of a semantically rich model with a high degree of temporal adaptability.

Ongoing interventions by private stakeholders can be integrated, improving prioritisation of district-scale conservation strategies. Moreover, the system is designed to be user-friendly, allowing local administrators to update and modify the models independently, without requiring advanced IT skills or external technical support.

An additional component of the proposed framework is the remote exploration of historic districts through digital models developed using Virtual Reality (VR) techniques. This addresses the frequent lack of digitised representations of historic urban areas, which—due to their distinctive morpho-typological features—require dedicated acquisition and processing protocols. In this context, the use of virtual models generated from spherical imagery emerges as an effective and intelligent tool for the rapid documentation of real environments. These models enable continuous visualisation and full spatial exploration across all phases, eliminating the need for repeated on-site surveys by the same operator and reducing the logistical complexity of involving multiple actors. Moreover, the integration of VR techniques facilitates collaborative knowledge sharing among the various stakeholders involved in the conservation process. The virtualisation of cultural heritage has demonstrated strong potential for linking 3D models to external structured databases, thereby enabling coherent information management and providing semi-structured support for technical diagnostics. The resulting relational database (r-DB) was tested in alignment with this objective, confirming its consistency with the traditional workflows and practices of conservation professionals.

Among the various approaches to generating digital models, the use of structured ontologies stands out for its capacity to enhance traditional procedures. This ensures the universality and autonomy of technical knowledge, while also enabling the extension of analyses to encompass thematic domains. The integration of CityGML with ontological structures facilitates the development of comprehensive digital recovery plans enriched with detailed semantic information, promoting a holistic understanding of historical, architectural, and environmental urban dimensions, and improving conservation strategy interoperability.

The developed digital code of practice has demonstrated significant potential in extending the CityGML data structure to encompass all relevant data classes associated with existing architectural heritage, as well as the full range of phases involved in the conservation process. The effectiveness and applicability of the digital code were validated through its experimental implementation across two pilot case studies. While sharing comparable historical, architectural, and constructional features, the cases presented distinct conservation challenges, allowing a comprehensive evaluation of the code's adaptability and robustness in addressing context-specific criticalities.

References

1. Batchelor D, Schnabel MA (2020) Interdisciplinary relationships, influence, and aspirations for smart heritage in local government. Heritage 3:1402–1415
2. Giuliani F, De Falco A, Cutini V, Di Sivo M (2021) A simplified methodology for risk analysis of historic centers: the world heritage site of San Gimignano, Italy. Int J Disaster Resil Built Environ 12:336–354. https://doi.org/10.1108/IJDRBE-04-2020-0029
3. Banfi F (2021) The evolution of interactivity, immersion and interoperability in HBIM: digital model uses, VR and AR for built cultural heritage. ISPRS Int J Geo-Inf 10:685
4. Yang X, Grussenmeyer P, Koehl M et al (2020) Review of built heritage modelling: integration of HBIM and other information techniques. J Cult Herit 46:350–360. https://doi.org/10.1016/j.culher.2020.05.008
5. Baik A (2024) A comprehensive heritage BIM methodology for digital modelling and conservation of built heritage: application to Ghiqa historical market, Saudi Arabia. Remote Sens 16:2833
6. Bruno N, Rechichi F, Achille C et al (2020) Integration of historical GIS data in a HBIM system. Int Arch Photogramm Remote Sens Spat Inf Sci XLIII-B4-2:427–434. https://doi.org/10.5194/isprs-archives-XLIII-B4-2020-427-2020
7. Aloshan M, Elghonaimy I, Mesbah E et al (2024) Strategies for the preservation of historic areas within existing middle Eastern cities: the case of historic Jeddah. Buildings 14:717
8. Alba-Rodríguez MD, Martínez-Rocamora A, González-Vallejo P et al (2017) Building rehabilitation versus demolition and new construction: economic and environmental assessment. Environ Impact Assess Rev 66:115–126. https://doi.org/10.1016/j.eiar.2017.06.002
9. Amato A, Andreoli M, Rovai M (2021) Adaptive reuse of a historic building by introducing new functions: a scenario evaluation based on participatory MCA applied to a former Carthusian Monastery in Tuscany, Italy. Sustainability 13:2335
10. Borri A, Corradi M (2019) Architectural heritage: a discussion on conservation and safety. Heritage 2:631–647
11. Kioussi A, Karoglou M, Labropoulos K et al (2013) Integrated documentation protocols enabling decision making in cultural heritage protection. J Cult Herit 14:e141–e146
12. Giuliani F, Gaglio F, Martino M, De Falco A (2024) A HBIM pipeline for the conservation of large-scale architectural heritage: the city walls of Pisa. Herit Sci 12:35. https://doi.org/10.1186/s40494-024-01141-4
13. Wardekker A, Nath S, Handayaningsih TU (2023) The interaction between cultural heritage and community resilience in disaster-affected volcanic regions. Environ Sci Policy 145:116–128. https://doi.org/10.1016/j.envsci.2023.04.008
14. Alavian Sadr M, Izadi MS, Shahabian P, Talebian MH (2021) Integrated conservation and development planning of urban spaces based on components of historic urban landscape. Athar 42
15. Colucci E, de Ruvo V, Lingua A et al (2020) HBIM-GIS integration: from IFC to cityGML standard for damaged cultural heritage in a multiscale 3D GIS. Appl Sci 10:1356. https://doi.org/10.3390/app10041356
16. Vandesande A, van Balen K, Della Torre S, Cardoso F (2018) Preventive and planned conservation as a new management approach for built heritage: from a physical health check to empowering communities and activating (lost) traditions for local sustainable development. J Cult Herit Manag Sustain Dev 8:78–81. https://doi.org/10.1108/JCHMSD-05-2018-076
17. Abdul Huq S, Puthuvayi B (2024) Assessing the performance of urban heritage conservation projects—influencing factors, aspects and priority weights. Built Herit 8:4. https://doi.org/10.1186/s43238-024-00116-5
18. Sapay SV, Abadi KPW, Kusuma GCW, Islamiaty NJF (2025) Heritage building conservation: sustainable and digital modelling, edited by Mohamed Marzouk. London: Routledge, 2023. eBook ISBN 9781003357483. Built Herit 9:39. https://doi.org/10.1186/s43238-025-00207-x

19. Damas Mollá L, Sagarna M, Zabaleta A et al (2022) Methodology for assessing the vulnerability of built cultural heritage. Sci Total Environ 845:157314. https://doi.org/10.1016/j.scitotenv.2022.157314
20. Penjor T, Banihashemi S, Hajirasouli A, Golzad H (2024) Heritage building information modeling (HBIM) for heritage conservation: Framework of challenges, gaps, and existing limitations of HBIM. Digit Appl Archaeol Cult Herit 35:e00366. https://doi.org/10.1016/j.daach.2024.e00366
21. Acampa G, Battisti F, Grasso M (2023) An evaluation system to optimize the management of interventions in the historic center of florence world heritage site: from building preservation to block refurbishment. Land 12:726

MIX
Papier aus verantwortungsvollen Quellen
Paper from responsible sources
FSC® C105338

If you have any concerns about our products,
you can contact us on
ProductSafety@springernature.com

In case Publisher is established outside the EU,
the EU authorized representative is:
Springer Nature Customer Service Center GmbH
Europaplatz 3, 69115 Heidelberg, Germany

Printed by Libri Plureos GmbH
in Hamburg, Germany